MW00884150

Heal Them All

by
Rev. Cheryl Schang

PRESS

This book is dedicated to two special people

My Father, Rev. Grant Aldridge,
who taught me to look beyond
the surface of the words in the
Bible to find the deeper meaning,
the treasures hidden in plain
sight.

My Pastor, Bishop Paul Zink,
who taught me to believe sickness
and disease is not from God and
it is God's will to heal us all.

Table of Contents

INTRODUCTION to the Healing Ministry *9*
The Ancient Door *11*
Tim's Story *19*

SECTION 1 – Healing for the Believer *23*
Wounded For Your Healing *25*
Road Blocks to Healing *33*

SECTION 2 – The Role of Faith *51*
Got Faith? *53*
The Prayer of Faith *73*
Use Someone Else's Faith *77*
The Breath of God *81*

SECTION 3 – Fixing the Error *85*
Problem Scriptures – Old Testament *121*
Problem Scriptures – New Testament *123*
Paul's Thorn *145*

SECTION 4 - Enemy Intelligence Briefing *121*
The Agreement That Cost You Your Health *123*
Breaking the Agreement *145*
Body-Soul Connection *175*
Other, Not So Obvious, Causes of Sickness *185*

SECTION 5 - How to Heal *189*
The Healing Process *191*
Thanksgiving *205*

Introduction to the Healing Ministry

The Ancient Door

I was in a prayer meeting years ago, long before I had imagined a healing ministry. As I prayed, I saw a vision that dramatically changed my life, although I did not fully understand it at the time. It was years later that I understood the connection between this vision and healing. Even to this day, I think the implications go far beyond a healing ministry and touch on other treasures of our spiritual inheritance.

In the vision, I saw myself standing on an ancient cobblestone street in a two thousand year old city. It was a marvelous scene. The street was lined with houses and shops. There was little color in the scene. Most everything was the color of rough hewn wood.

Perhaps that is why the doors at the end of the street were so noticeable. They were huge, gold, shiny doors. The doors were closed, but I could see through them, as though the gold were transparent.

I could see many beautiful objects beyond the doors: golden goblets, golden platters, and objects for which I have no words.

"What is this?" I asked the Lord.

"It is a legitimate door of ministry," He said. He did not

need to speak more. I knew He was offering me this type of ministry.

Since my curiosity was aroused, I decided to look around some more before accepting. I focused my attention back on the ancient lane. As I studied it more carefully, I noticed another doorway to my right. It was exactly the opposite of the large golden doors. I call it a doorway, for there was no door.

Although there was no door, I could not see in. It was totally dark inside and the darkness hid the interior. The frame of the opening was not straight. The threshold was nothing but dust and rotted boards – quite unappealing to the casual observer. It looked as though the place had been left to deteriorate.

"What is this?" I asked the Lord.

He answered, "It is another legitimate door of ministry. It's the ancient way. Which will you choose?" The vision ended.

I was intrigued by this vision for many weeks. Each time I thought of it, I was struck by the contrasts: A door that was golden versus a doorway that was dirt and wood. The beautiful door was closed and the doorway was open for all who would come. The closed door was transparent. The ancient doorway did not have a door; yet, I could not see inside to know what lay beyond.

Many months later, I was in prayer again when the vision reappeared. I hadn't thought about it in quite a while. In the vision I was standing at the opening of the little ancient doorway. I told the Lord I wanted to choose the ancient way. I started to enter, but the opening for the doorway was so low that I had to bow to get in. The symbolism of that was not lost on me. I realized the Lord was telling me that I had to enter with a bowed spirit, a spirit of humility.

I entered a room that was actually more like a cave than a room. It was extremely dark, and it took a few moments for my eyes to adjust. I began to notice that there were little streams of light coming in through the doorway. As my eyes adjusted, I could see that everything around me looked old and forgotten. It almost appeared as if no one had ever been there; yet, I could feel that others had been there before me, but not for hundreds of years.

I looked at the soft floor of dirt. The shafts of light were catching something which sparkled in the dust. I reached down and picked up one of the sparking items. It was a fabulous gemstone as large as a grapefruit. It was already cut and polished, an awesome sight.

A thousand questions raced through my mind. How could it be that no one had discovered such a treasure of great worth? There was no door to keep people out. How could the owner let it lay in the dust? As my eyes adjusted to this strange environment, I noticed there were other such stones lying in the dust. I stood there speechless.

The Lord said, "These are my ancient treasures." I still did not know what He meant. What exactly did these treasures represent? Without realizing it, my arm had begun to ache from the weight of the gemstone. Before I could say anything, God addressed this thought: "Yes, it's a weighty matter to hold my treasures." The vision ended.

I had some ideas about the whole interpretation, but it wasn't until I started ministering in the area of healing that I began to understand about the ancient way and the treasures of great weight. The golden door was a legitimate door of ministry. It was flashy and glitzy. It was the kind of healing ministry I was being offered. We all know, or know of, people in this kind of healing ministry. There are legitimate faith healers whose ministries bring in multi-million of dollars a year. They can pack an auditorium to the point where people are beating down the doors. People legitimately get healed. This is a very glamorous kind of ministry. It was represented by the golden door.

Jesus' ministry was not so glamorous. No one paid him millions of dollars a year to do it. We have no record of mass healings in the ministry of Jesus. I might wish this were not so, but the model that Jesus used is slow and arduous work. He taught the masses, but apparently healed them one by one. He allowed Himself to be touched by the people and by their humanity.

In later years I once complained to God that it sometimes takes us two hours to get someone healed. I wanted the microwave version of healing.

"Isn't there a faster way?" I asked.

The Lord reminded me that I had chosen the ancient doorway. I was permitted to hold those ancient treasures that have been lying in the dust for thousands of years.

I would love to have a quick, easy solution to each person's illness. I would rather not get involved with all of their problems and issues. But then there would not be much difference between this and the "golden door" ministries, where some are healed and some are not. The Lord showed me that by choosing the ancient way we could "**heal them all**" just as Jesus did.

I had been given the answer to the burning question of my soul. Have you ever thought of the one question you would ask Jesus if you could ask him only one thing? My question was, *"How did Jesus heal them all?"* I had seen that we could get a few sick people healed here and there from time to time, but the truth is that we did not know what we did right when it happened, and we did not know what we did wrong when it did not happen.

There was no repeatable process; so what was the secret? **How did He do it every time with no failures – a 100% success rate?**

As I thought about the differences between the method of healing I will teach you in this book and the method of healing that is used by some world famous faith healers, I realized that my answer lay in those differences.

When a healing minister calls out an illness and some get healed and some do not, there are several things operating. First, the minister is expecting the people to use their own faith. They must claim that word and reach out and take it. The minister on the platform usually does not pray for them personally until after they're healed. So, if you come with your own faith and get a revelation, you can reach out and receive your healing. Yet, that does not explain all the difference.

Two people can have the same disease, with the same amount of faith (it only takes a tiny amount), yet one is healed and the other is not. For the one that is not healed, we have come to understand that there is something blocking the healing. In this case, an extra step is required.

Then there are some that are healed in these meetings, but don't stay healed. What's up with that? Did God's power wear off? No, **the answer is that they got a breakthrough without dealing with the root cause of the illness.** They soon returned to the behaviors or thoughts that produced the illness and the symptoms returned. The key is to get to the root. **What has blocked the glory?**

I respect the differences in healing ministries. I thank God for every one of them out there doing this work. They are providing hope and healing power to many. My approach is not glamorous. It is slow work, built on relationship, care, and love. It does not give you the luxury of standing at a distance and never becoming involved with the person who needs your help. By following His method, The Ancient Way, you will be able bring healing to those that come to you earnestly desiring to be healed. **If they will do whatever it takes and you will do whatever it takes, you are going to see predictable, repeatable results.**

Everywhere I teach, people ask me how I got started in the healing ministry. I am sure they want to know if some lightning from heaven came and hit me, or if some angel appeared with a vile of oil. Do I have some special anointing? The answer is no. I have nothing special except the Holy Spirit, the same Holy Spirit you have. I just had my eyes opened to the power that is available to us because we have the Holy Spirit. Here is the story of how I learned.

Several years ago, I took the summer off and began to pray, fast, study, and research healing in the Bible. I wasn't really getting any breakthrough. I learned a few things, but I really had more questions than answers.

Finally, I said to God, "I know I just picked this topic. Maybe you don't really want me to learn about healing. Maybe it's not the right time. Do you want me to stop?" At the time I didn't hear Him say anything.

Shortly after that, I was driving down the road and I heard the Lord say to me, "Last Rites."

Sounded weird to me, but that's what I heard: "Last Rites." The only thing I knew about "Last Rites" was that it is something the Catholic Church gave to people who were dying. Not being Catholic, I didn't understand why I was hearing these words. I thought maybe God was telling me someone was going to die. I finally decided I must have heard wrong and tossed the thought aside.

A few weeks later, I was still studying, pressing in, praying, and making little progress. I knew there was revelation that I was missing, and it felt like I just could not get a breakthrough.

I prayed again: "God, should I give up? Should I not be doing this? It just doesn't seem to be clicking for me."

That's when I heard the Lord shout, "Last Rites." Suddenly, I knew I was to learn to do "Last Rites."

I didn't know how to do this, so I called a friend of mine who used to be a Catholic nun.

I said to her, "Don't tell anybody, but God told me I'm supposed to learn how to do Last Rites. Is there a book I can read to learn how to do it?

She started laughing. She said, "Cheryl, we don't call it Last Rites anymore. It is now called the 'Sacrament of Healing.' We don't give it to people who are dying. We give it to people who are sick."

God used this strange, round-about, prophetic word to encourage me. Now I knew without a doubt that God was saying, "Yes, I want you to learn healing."

Because of this word of encouragement, I continued my study thorough out the summer.

As I studied, the words of the prophet who had trained me in prophetic ministry kept coming back to me over and over again: "If you don't know how to do the prophetic, you can't do the other stuff."

In light of this revelation, John 5:30 really came alive to me: "*I can of mine own self do nothing: as I hear, I judge: and my judgment is just; because I seek not mine own will, but the will of the Father which hath sent me.*" **Jesus only said what He heard the Father say.** When I put these two revelations together, I began to understand that Jesus had a *rhema* word (a specific word from God for that particular situation) for everyone He healed.

I had been looking for a pattern or a formula. I had studied every account of Jesus healing someone, yet I could find no common thread. One time He spit and made mud. Another time He said, "Take up your bed and walk." Yet another time He said, "Your sins are forgiven." Many times He healed someone by casting out a demon. It seemed like there was no pattern; but actually there was. **He had a *rhema* word for each case.** Jesus knew what the voice of God sounded like on the inside of Him. He spoke the words needed for each particular situation.

One of the first stories of healing in the Bible has to do with a situation between Abraham and Abimelech. There was a curse of barrenness on all of Abimelech's household.

God told Abimelech to return Sarah to Abraham and that Abraham was a prophet and he would pray for him.[1] It is just like God to hide this little treasure in plain sight. During Old Testament times, God usually only spoke directly to kings, priests, and prophets. It makes sense that Abraham could heal Abimelech because he was a prophet. That meant that he could hear from God exactly what needed to be said or done in that situation.

These pages contain the revelation the Lord gave me that summer; a way to defeat sickness and disease in the lives of believers. As you read, I pray that they will become *rhema* to you also.

---

[1] Genesis 20:7

Tim's Story

Building on the foundation of the prophetic, I started putting together my understanding of the scriptures on healing. When I got all done, I said, "Okay, God, I think I get it. But, before I can share this with anyone, I'd like You to prove to me this really works. If You will give me somebody who is almost dead and this really works, then I will know You have shown me the truth about healing. I appreciate the fact you heal someone's headache. But, I want You to give me somebody who is almost dead. Then I will know that no doctor, no pill, no man-made cure can take credit for the healing. Nothing will be able to take the credit except the truth You have shown me."

Two or three days later I was talking to a friend on the phone. During our conversation she said to me, "I wish you would pray for my friend at work. Her 20 year old son was hit by a truck. He is in the hospital. They have declared him brain dead. They have given the mother the form to sign to make him an organ donor. The family has already paid for the funeral. It's a sad situation."

I exclaimed, "Oh! He's almost dead!"

I think she was a little startled by my response.

I said, "We need to go pray for him. Can we pray for him today?"

We contacted the family and got their permission to go see him. When we got to the hospital, we worked our way into the critical care unit.

Tim had an infection. His back was broken. His pelvis was broken in five places. His brain was swollen. They had not even bothered to set the bones in his body because, technically, his brain was dead. Nothing was working. The machines alone were keeping him alive.

As we prayed, we asked God to give us a *rhema* word. We said, "God, what is the one thing you want us to declare and pray today?"

He spoke a word to us and we declared what He said.

While we there the young man's vital signs changed. We told the mother that the Bible says, "lay hands on the sick and they will recover." Recovery is a process. We asked her to please give it 24 to 48 hours before giving the okay to unplug the machines. We told her something would change.

She said, "If he would just open his eyes, I would know."

We prayed and asked that God would open his eyes as a sign for the mother. Sure enough, about 48 hours later, one eye popped open. The doctors said it meant nothing, but to the mother it was a sign. After that, no one could convince the mother to unplug him.

Over a period of six weeks, we prayed for him several more times. Each time God gave us a *rhema* word, a word of knowledge. We cast out demonic powers, we remitted sins, we commanded his body in various ways to heal. Each time there was progress in his condition. We never saw the change when we prayed. It always seemed like it was 24-48 hours after we prayed that the thing for which we prayed manifest.

Six weeks from the time we walked into the ICU in that hospital (the funeral was paid for and doctors were wanting to harvest the organs) that young man was up walking, talking, seeing, and every bone in his body miraculously healed. He still needed rehab, but he was well on the way. Thank You God! I now know healing is real, and the truths You have shown me really work.

Now, I need to tell you that one day, after going to the hospital to pray for Tim, I was driving home pondering the events of the day. I had heard that there might have been alcohol involved in the accident. I began to worry. What if I was helping to get someone healed who would get drunk and sit behind the wheel of a car? Next time, he might hit and kill a child.

I cried out to God. "Lord, how will I know if I am supposed to heal someone? What if they are bad people and the healing would bring misery to others? What if they live only to hurt other innocent people? Lord, how will I know?"

I heard the Lord clearly say that I was treading on His territory. It was not up to me to meddle in such things. Then I heard those precious words that have become the title for this book. He said, "**Heal them all!**"

Praying for people and seeing them healed is the inheritance of every believer. I don't have some special anointing from God. I didn't have some unusual event happen in my life. I have not known since I was a child that I was going to be involved in a healing ministry. One day I just said, "God, I believe your word on healing is true. Show me how it works," and He did!

Words that the prophet who trained me had spoken to me proved to be true: "If you don't know what the voice of God sounds like on the inside of you, you can't do the other stuff."

Hearing the voice of God is important to us in every area of our life. It is critical in the ministry of healing. It is the key to "healing them all" as you find out from the many stories of healing you will read in these pages.

Over the years, I have trained hundreds of people to listen for the *rhema*, use that *rhema* to remove the blockage, and bring healing to people all over the world. We now have a school in Jacksonville, Florida, where we train people in the principles we used to minister to Tim. These principles are also contained in this book.

During the summer I studied healing, I made a promise to God. "Lord, if you will give me the understanding of healing, I will not keep it for myself. I promise I will share it with anyone who will listen!" This book is the fulfillment of that promise I made to the Lord.

This book was designed to serve two purposes. It provides a theological foundation for the claim that it is God's will that all be healed. Then it provides a step by step set of instructions for obtaining healing for yourself and for ministering healing to others.

Section 1

Healing
For The Believer

Wounded For Your Healing

Hidden in plain view in the scriptures is an amazing truth:

Jesus did not just die
that you might live,
He was also wounded
that you might be healed.

Through the death of Jesus, we have eternal life. No Christian disputes this truth. There is another powerful truth that has been distorted and lost over the years. It is this: He was wounded so that you could be physically and emotionally healed in this lifetime.

The Old Testament is full of types and shadows of God's plan for the redemption of man. God often veiled His plans in a mystery so that man could know them only by revelation of the Holy Spirit. In 1 Corinthians 2:6-8 Paul tells us why God did it this way.

How is it we speak wisdom among them that are perfect; yet not the wisdom of this world, nor of the princes of this world, that come to nought: But we speak the wisdom of God in a mystery, even the hidden wisdom, which God ordained before the world unto our glory: Which none of the princes of this world knew: for had they known it, they would not have crucified the Lord of glory.

How could Satan and the princes of this world not have known God's plan of redemption? We know that Satan must have read the scriptures because he quoted them (albeit incorrectly) to Jesus when he tempted Him in the wilderness.[2]

He knew the scriptures, but because he did not have the Holy Spirit to bring revelation with that Word, there was no understanding. It was veiled to him. Paul said if it had not been veiled in a mystery, Satan would have figured out that he'd better not allow Jesus to be crucified.

To fully understand the Word of God one must have the inspiration of the Holy Spirit. Only then can we fully understand the symbols and what they foretold. These symbols are referred to as types and shadows.

The sacrificial offerings of Israel were symbolic. They symbolized the sacrifice of Jesus. By studying those sacrifices, we can learn much about what was accomplished by Jesus' sacrifice.

There is a surprising revelation for us when we consider the sacrifices that were offered for redemption. Jesus perfectly fulfilled all the types and shadows of the sacrificial offerings with one exception.

In ancient Israel, the sacrificial lamb had to be without spot or blemish.[3] It had to come to the altar without a mark on it. We know that this is not a picture of how our Savior came to the cross. He was morally spotless, but his exterior did not match the picture of the Passover lamb. He was tortured and mutilated before his death more than any other man.[4]

Also, when a lamb was offered as a sacrifice, it was killed in the most humane way. The lamb's throat was cut so the blood could to be collected in a basin. In this manner of death, the lamb lost consciousness and died without trauma. As we know, that does not match the picture of Jesus' experience. He did not die a painless death.

Why the deviation? The truth is that **Jesus could have died a painless death to give you eternal life.** All that was required was His life in exchange for yours. He could have fulfilled the type and shadow of the sacrifices without suffering. He could have completed the plan for your eternal life without the scourge of the Roman whip. He could have just died, so that you could live eternally. But He didn't. **He was wounded so that you could be healed.** The prophet Isaiah foretold that He would do such a thing.

Do you understand that it was not His suffering that brought you eternal life? It was His death that brought you eternal life. His **suffering** brought your healing. *"By his stripes you are healed."*[5]

The Greek word *mastix* is translated "plagues," meaning physical sickness, three times. It is translated "scourgings," meaning to be beaten with a Roman whip, twice.[6] The *mastix* (the beating) was for the plagues or physical sickness.

Jesus did not just replace the Old Covenant with a New Covenant. He replaced it with a new and improved version.[7] This New Covenant had healing built into it.

In the Old Covenant, healing and health were conditional. If you read the promises in Deuteronomy 28, you will see that health (or lack of it) depended on obedience to the law. The Hebrews were not entitled to divine health just because they were people of God. Sin still had dominion over the things in this world.

Jesus' sacrifice didn't just provide us with an escape route to heaven. His work took back dominion. He came to restore what Adam had lost – dominion over the things in this realm. Whatever Jesus took to the cross, the power of it died with Him. **Whatever was on Jesus when He left this realm in**

death, the power of those things left this realm also.

Jesus took your sins to the cross with Him and therefore the power of sin is broken. He also, by the scourging of the Roman whip, took every sickness and disease that existed. The power of those things died with Jesus. **Whatever had power over you, Jesus now has power over it.** All Satan has left are lies. As a believer, you have been delegated the power that Jesus possesses. Since Satan has no power, he must get you to believe a lie so that you will use your power (in agreement with him) to bring something to pass. We will discuss this more thoroughly in the following chapters.

With this understanding, let's take a fresh look at three key verses concerning the full work of the atonement. The prophet Isaiah lived and prophesied seven to eight hundred years before Jesus was crucified. Although prophecies concerning the Messiah (Messianic prophecies) can be found as far back as Adam and Eve, none so fully details the promise of healing as those of Isaiah's. In the types and shadows of the Old Testament, one can find the hope of both redemption and healing. (ie. the brass serpent). None however, is as direct as Isaiah 53:4-5.

> *"Surely He has borne our griefs and carried our sorrows: yet we did esteem Him stricken, smitten of God and afflicted. But He was wounded for our transgressions, He was bruised for our iniquities: the chastisement of our peace was upon Him; and with His stripes we are healed."*

There are several words that need to be examined here because the full meaning is not clear in this King James translation. The first word is "griefs." This is the Hebrew word *kholee*, sometimes spelled *choliy*. According to Strong's Exhaustive Concordance, this word means malady, anxiety, or calamity and comes from the root word *chalah*, which means to be weak, sick, afflicted. This Hebrew word is used 22 times in the Old Testament, and every place it occurs (with the exception of Isaiah 53 and in the book of Jeremiah) it is translated either sickness or disease.[8]

The word "sorrows" in this passage of Isaiah is the Hebrew word, *makob*. It means anguish or affliction. It comes from the root word *ka'ab*, which means to feel pain. You can find this same Hebrew word translated as "pain" in Job 33:19 – *"He is chastened also with pain upon his bed."* And you can find it in Jeremiah 51:8 – *"Take balm for her pain."*[9] Therefore, this verse would be better translated: *"Surely he hath borne our sickness and carried our pain."*

Let's also examine the two verbs used here. The word "borne" is the Hebrew word *nasa*. This word is used 590 times in the Old Testament and is used both figuratively and literally.

The first time we find this word in Scripture, it is used by Cain in Genesis 4:13.[10] Cain said to the Lord, *"My punishment is greater than I can bear."* Clearly, Cain is talking about suffering punishment for something he did. The same is true of its use in Leviticus 5:1 – *"If a soul sin,...then he shall bear his iniquity."* This word, used in Isaiah 53:4 to describe the work of Jesus concerning healing, is the same word used just a few verses later, in verse 12, to describe the work of Jesus concerning sin: *"...and He bore the sin of many and made intercession for the transgressors."* This means **in the same way that Jesus bore your sins, He bore your sickness.**

The other verb in this passage is the Hebrew word *sabal*, (sometimes spelled *cabal*) which is translated as "carried." This is a good translation. Strong's gives the same translation for this word: to carry (literally or figuratively), to be burdensome. You can see it used in Lamentations 5:7 – *"Our fathers have sinned...and we have borne their iniquities."*

We can see that this word is also used consistently in

borne same "cabal"

Isaiah 53 to speak of sickness and sin. Verse 11 contains this word. Although it appears in the English as the word 'bear', it is the Hebrew word *sabal: "...for he shall bear their iniquities."* Again, the same word used to describe the work of Jesus concerning sickness (in verse 4) is used to describe His work concerning sin (in verse 11).

So, in this prophecy in Isaiah, we find that **to the same extent the Messiah would take our sin, He would take our sickness and pain.** Hundreds of years before the cross, the prophet had the revelation of the coming Messiah. Here it is plainly stated that the atonement was to include not only forgiveness of sins, but healing as well. It was always meant to be part of the same package. Since Jesus fulfilled this prophesy, the linkage between salvation and healing is sealed for all eternity. You cannot separate those two things.

There is evidence that the Jews living at the time of Jesus were familiar with this passage from Isaiah. In fact, more than just knowing it, they were anticipating the fulfillment of it. They knew it was a Messianic prophecy. Since they were looking for Messiah, they were looking for someone who would fit the description Isaiah offered of Messiah.

This match – the fact that Jesus fit Isaiah's description – was clear to the gospel writer, Matthew, and he makes note of it in his description of Jesus' ministry.

"When the evening was come they brought unto Him many that were possessed with devils and He cast the spirits out with His Word and healed all that were sick that it might be fulfilled which was spoken by Isaiah, the prophet, saying Himself took our infirmities and bare our sickness." [11]

Matthew was reminding them of the prophecy of Isaiah. He connected Jesus to this prophecy. By doing so, he identified the work of Jesus' ministry of healing and deliverance as the very work that was prophesied by Isaiah.

Isaiah saw the full work of the cross before it happened. Matthew identified the work of Jesus as that which was foretold by Isaiah.[12]

After Jesus left, the disciples taught that it was the same work of the cross, prophesied by Isaiah, and reported by Matthew, which was the basis for the ministry work of the believer. The apostle Peter made the connection for us. We find his words in 1 Peter 2:24. In this verse, Peter looks back at the cross after Jesus has gone to heaven and he reminds us of what is included in our package.

"Who His own self bore our sins in His body on the tree that we being dead to sins should live to righteousness by whose stripes you were healed."[13]

Did you notice that Peter spoke of this work in the past tense? Isaiah prophesied it before it happened. When Jesus was doing it, Matthew declared, "This is what it looks like." After Jesus was gone, Peter pointed back to the cross and he said, "That is what happened back there." In the very same breath Peter declared healing and salvation are in the same package.

---

[2] Luke 4

[3] Exodus 12:5

[4] Isaiah 52:14

[5] Isaiah 53:5

[6] Compare Mark 3:10, 5:29, 5:34 with Acts 22:24 and Hebrews 11:36

[7] Hebrews 8:6

[8] Bible Research Systems, Version 6.1 Revision A, Austin, Texas, 1995

[9] Ibid

[10] Ibid

[11] Matthew 8:16-17

[12] McCrossan, Dr. T.J., Bodily Healing and The Atonement, RHEMA Bible Church, Tulsa OK, 1982, 15-18 According to Dr. McCrossan, the word fulfilled is *plerothe*, the 1st Aorist passive, subjunctive, 3rd person singular of *pleroo*. It is the same word that appears in Matthew 12:17-21 where Matthew again quotes Isaiah and declares that the word foretold by the prophet in Isaiah 42:1-4 has been 'fulfilled'. The Aorist tense, which indicates momentary completed past action is also used to express future events which must certainly happen. So Matthew was saying that by these present actions of Jesus, we see that the rest of the word must certainly be fulfilled as well. Jesus also used this same word in the same tense when he (in Luke 4:21) took the Scriptures and read from Isaiah and declared that the scripture had been 'fulfilled' that day. Yet, there the work was not finished that day, but because he had started, it will be completed.

[13] 1 Peter 2:24

Road Bocks to Healing

Can you remember the time when you were born again? Did a certificate fall from heaven with God's signature on it? No? Did anything change on the outside? Did your hair change color? Did you grow? Did you shrink? Did you lose weight? Did you gain weight? No?

Well, how do you know that you are saved? Sounds like faith, right? You just believe that you are saved? All you have as proof of your eternal life is the witness of the Holy Spirit, and the Word of God. On this evidence alone, you have made an eternal decision. You required no other proof. Wow!

Since healing and eternal salvation are in the same package, you are going to get your healing the same way. Furthermore, **the same things that blocked your salvation before you got saved are the same things that can block your healing before you get healed**.

For the purposes of this book, I have put these things which can block your healing into four categories. I admit there is no scriptural basis for these categories. I just created them so it would be easier to remember them. First let me identify them, and then we will discuss how to deal with them.

of categories

➢ **Ignorance**. You just don't know or haven't been taught or exposed to a truth. When it came to your salvation, you did not know that Jesus died for your sins. You learned what He did because someone taught you. Because someone proclaimed truth to you, the ignorance was destroyed.

Ignorance can also block your healing; you just don't know that you are entitled to be healed. Maybe somewhere along the line someone taught you incorrectly because of their own ignorance. Therefore, you just do not know that it is your right to be healed.

God, by the work of the Holy Spirit, gave us His word in written form. It's called the Bible. God did not write it because He thought He might forget what He had said. He wrote it so you could know. He gave us His word in written form so that we would not be ignorant.

When we learn about God and His provisions for us through His word, we destroy the ignorance that has blocked our healing. I am going to destroy some of it right now.

We just read Isaiah 53:4-5. Do you remember the phrase, *"Surely he has borne our griefs and carried our sorrows?"* Here is the good news. Not only did He take your sickness, but your pain as well. **Jesus already took your pain, and there is no reason for both of you to have it.** You have the right to be free from pain, as well as sickness and disease.

By His stripes you were healed. That word "healed" is the Hebrew word *rapha*. It means to mend, to cure, to make whole. In the Hebrew language it is the same word as "physician." So don't let anyone mislead you into thinking this word only means spiritual healing. You don't hire a physician to heal your spirit. It is **physical** healing.

34

By examining the Septuagint (the Greek translation of the entire Bible), you can see a consistency in the terminology that is not quite so evident in the English. The Greek word for "healed" in Isaiah 53:5 is *iaomai*.[14] This word speaks of physical healing in the New Testament.

Your healing is in the atonement. **If you are born again you have the right to be healed. It is in the same package.**

We read Matthew 8:16-17 previously. In that passage, Matthew described the work of Jesus and made the connection to Isaiah. Matthew informed us that people brought those who were possessed with the devil and those who were sick to Jesus, and Jesus treated them both the same. He healed them!

As a matter of fact, there are five words in the Greek that are translated into English as "healed," or "heal." In every case they are used both for physical healing and deliverance (casting out demons) indiscriminately.

This means that when Jesus ministered to someone, He didn't care whether they were paralyzed because they had a disease or a demon. He recognized the work of the enemy and He came to destroy the work of the enemy.[15] **Much of the time when Jesus "healed" someone, He was casting out a demon.**

This is a point we will discuss in detail later, but just let me say that I don't believe that Christians can be demon possessed. Possession is about ownership, and you have been bought with a price.

However, we come to the Lord with a lot of baggage. For years we let stuff (anger, fear, rejection etc.) get in our souls. When your spirit was born again your soul still had all that stuff in it. The stuff doesn't own you, but it sure causes a problem for you; and it can cause your disease or block your healing.

Jesus healed them all. These words from Matthew 8:16 hooked me years ago. **Jesus healed them all.** I would read it over and over again. Every time I studied healing, I kept bumping into this fact – Jesus healed them all. I thought there must be some catch, so I looked it up.

What does this word "all" mean? Maybe it means that He healed so many of them that you might as well say "all." Maybe it means He healed "nearly all" of them, so let's just call it "all."

But here is the truth: it is the Greek word *pas*. It means all, any, every, the whole, everyone, everyway, thoroughly, whatsoever, whosoever. Does that sound like "all" to you? It sounds like "all" to me.

Matthew quoted Isaiah 53 and told us that in the casting out of demons and the physical healing of the sick the promise is realized. Remember also that when Peter wrote about healing, it was in the past tense.

> *Who his own self bare our sins in his own body on the tree, that we, being dead to sins, should live unto righteousness: by whose stripes you were healed.*

The word "our" in this verse is the Greek word *hemon*. It means that **Christ took the infirmities and sicknesses of the very same persons for whose sins He died.**[16] Not different people or a part of the people, but the very same people for whom He died. Remember that.

Is the ignorance destroyed? Do you know for certain that healing is in the atonement package? If not, reread those passages in Isaiah, Matthew and Peter.

➤ **Unbelief**. The second thing that blocks your salvation, and can block your healing, is unbelief. You may say, "Yes, I know God can save some people, but I am just not really sure that God wants to save me. You just don't know how bad I am. You don't know the sins that I have committed. I am not certain that it applies to me." That attitude will block your salvation.

That same flawed logic will block your healing. It is easy for us to see the flaw in the logic when we are talking about salvation, right? We would never think that one is beyond salvation or that salvation only applies to some people. We believe that it is God's will that all should be saved.[17] Salvation is not for a few, and it is not based on works or whether we deserve it. It is offered to all.

It's the same for your healing. Healing and salvation come in the same package. They are inseparable. You wonder if it is God's will to heal you. You're not sure. Let's destroy that thinking now.

Jesus came to destroy the works of the enemy - 1 John 3:8. **You can tell the things that Jesus considered a work of the enemy (not a work of God) by what He destroyed.** You can make a broad statement and say that Jesus came to destroy sin. However, the ministry of Jesus seems to have been focused on destroying three specific manifestations of sin: false teaching, demonic oppression, and sickness/disease. Everywhere Jesus went He cast out demons. Therefore the work of demons in a person's life must be the work of the enemy. It is not in the Kingdom of God.

Is sin in the Kingdom of God? No? Then Jesus came to destroy that didn't He? Is there sickness and disease in the Kingdom of God? Maybe some of you are not so sure about the answer to that last question. Let me ask this: Were Adam and Eve created with sickness and disease? Do you expect to be sick in heaven? Most would answer no to this question.

We know that sickness and death entered the earth with sin. **Sin and sickness are connected just like salvation**

and healing are connected. Therefore, we can determine that sickness is from the enemy, and Jesus came to destroy the works of the enemy.

Jesus healed all who were oppressed by the devil.[18] This Greek word translated "oppressed" is *katadunasteuomenous*. It means to dominate or exercise lordship over. If you have sin, if you have allowed some demonic force to have power in your life, if you have sickness, then you are oppressed by the devil and he is exercising lordship over some aspect of your life. Jesus came to destroy these works of the enemy.

According to Acts 10:38, healing is the cure for oppression. That means that healing is what is needed when someone is oppressed by the enemy. This is one more proof that Jesus treated healing physical sickness and casting out a demon as the same work.

Jesus said that a kingdom divided cannot stand.[19] Now if sickness is of the Kingdom of God, and Jesus went around healing people, then the Kingdom of God must be divided, right?

But we know that the Kingdom of God is **not** divided, and sickness and disease is **not** of the Kingdom of God. Bitter water and sweet water do not come from the same source.[20]

God is not the source of sickness and disease. He didn't create it. He is the Creator and He is Omnipotent – all powerful – and He could have created anything! He chose **not** to create sickness and disease. It is **not** consistent with His nature and character.

Sickness and disease is a product of the fall. It is the work of the enemy of your soul. So why would God take something that was created by His enemy to put it on somebody? Isn't that a foolish idea?

Yet, there was a doctrine that went around for awhile that said that God puts sickness and disease on you to teach you something. Since God didn't create it, it means He would have to borrow it from Satan in order to put it on you. How profoundly insane that sounds!

How was God going to ever teach Adam and Eve anything in the garden before the fall if this was His only way of teaching them something? Maybe He just planned to talk to them. And that is how He teaches us today – by His Word, by His *rhema.* I will discuss this in more detail in another chapter.

Jesus healed them all! We are at a crossroads here. **Jesus healed them all**; every time, always, everyone, whosoever, whatsoever, totally, wholly, completely, thoroughly – He healed them all.

Now if it is not God's will for all of them to be healed, was Jesus in rebellion? Jesus was not in rebellion because it is God's will to heal every single time: ALL – everyone, everybody, everywhere, whosoever, whatsoever, in every circumstance, totally, thoroughly, completely.

Paul said in his letter to the Romans, *This same spirit that raised Jesus from the dead quickens your mortal bodies.*[21] The word 'quicken' here is a verb in the Greek; it comes from the word, *zoë,* meaning "life", and *poieo,* which means "I make." So, **it is the work of the Holy Spirit to keep making life in these mortal bodies.**

If God doesn't want to heal you, then is the Holy Spirit in rebellion? Can you even imagine the Holy Spirit being in rebellion?

Imagine the Holy Spirit saying, "Okay Father, I know you don't want to heal this person, but it is my job to keep making life in them."

How absurd! I can't even imagine it. The Holy Spirit is not in rebellion. **It is the Holy Spirit's job to keep making life in us because it's the will of Father God.**

Romans 8:26 tells us that the Holy Spirit "helps our infirmities." This word "helps" is the Greek word *sunantilambanomai,* and it means "to take hold together with us against the thing."

The Holy Spirit comes along side you when you have an infirmity (feebleness of body or soul) and locks arms with you to stand against that thing. The Holy Spirit says, "Okay, come on; we are going to do this together. I am going to take hold with you against this sickness."

Now, if it is not God's will to heal you every single time, I guess the Holy Spirit has a lot of explaining to do! But we know it is God's will to heal you every single time. The Holy Spirit is not in rebellion to the Godhead. Jesus ministered by the power of the Holy Spirit and consistently, Jesus healed them all.

Satan comes to kill, steal and destroy, and Jesus came that you might have life more abundantly.[22] How abundant can your life be if you are sick?

Is Jesus messing up? Is He not doing His job? Perhaps that is what some of you think. "I am sick, so Jesus has not done His part."

For much of the rest of this book, I will show you that God has done His part, Jesus has done His part, and the Holy Spirit stands ready to do His part. **The only one that still has not done his part is you.** That is good news. This means that the help you need is within your own grasp.

Jesus also healed as proof that He had power to forgive sins. Jesus said, *"But that you may know that the Son of Man has authority on earth to forgive sins..."* He said to the paralytic, *"I tell you, get up, take your mat and go home."*[23]

That's the same reason that He heals today; because He has forgiven your sins. It's in your contract. The Word of God is your contract with God. He wrote it down for you so you could know what to expect, and know all your entitlements. The Bible is a copy of your contract, your covenant with God. Healing is a provision of your contract. He forgave your sins, so that means He heals you as well. It is written in the same clause in your contract.

Many have made up a lot of excuses to explain their failures and have called it God. In Matthew 17, we read of the disciples being sent out to heal, to raise the dead, to cast out demons, and to cleanse the leper. When they couldn't cast the demon out of a boy, they came back to Jesus and asked, "Why couldn't we do it?"

I was once driving down the street, and the Lord said, "Do you remember that time when the disciples came and asked Jesus why they couldn't cast out the demon?"

I said, "Yes, Lord."

He asked, "Well, do you remember what I identified as the problem?"

I answered, "Of course! You said this kind only comes out by prayer and fasting."

He said, "No, I didn't."

I insisted, "Yes you did, I am pretty sure that's what you said."

Well, I wasn't remembering the complete version given in Matthew 17, because there, Jesus said, "Oh you couldn't cast them out? It's because of your unbelief. If you only have faith the size of a mustard seed you could say to this mountain, ..." Then He said, "*this kind only comes out by prayer and fasting.*"

Suppose Jesus had already gone back to Heaven and the disciples had encountered this demon they couldn't cast out – do you think perhaps they would have made up a doctrine of why it didn't work? "Well, you know Jesus really doesn't want to cast this kind of demon out every time. You know God is sovereign and it is His will and we just have to find out if maybe He wants to do it this time."

Does that sound familiar? We have made up doctrines and excuses to explain our own failures.

If you read the message behind the message in this story, Jesus was saying: **It is the job of the minister to have the**

faith. If you are going to be the one standing there declaring deliverance and healing, you'd better have some faith yourself. You can't count on the person who is receiving ministry to have the faith. You'd better get your own.

We have said to people who are sick, "Oh, if you just have enough faith…" and, when they didn't get healed, we have said, "You must not have enough faith."

I say what Jesus said to those disciples: "Minister, Look at yourself!"

I tell those to whom I am ministering, "If you don't get healed, it's because I don't have enough faith since I am the minister. It has nothing to do with your faith if I am the one laying hands on you. It is very nice if you have faith. It helps me out and I don't have to work as hard. But it is my job, as the one ministering, to be the one with the faith."

Jesus clearly put the responsibility on the disciples because of their unbelief. I will discuss the minister's faith more in a later section.

 ➤ **Spiritual Interference.** The third thing that can block your salvation and also block your healing is spiritual interference – more precisely, demonic interference, generational curses and things like this. The enemy interferes with a person's ability to know the truth by blinding them spiritually.[24] That truth has the ability to set a person free, spiritually speaking.[25]

The same thing is true for healing. The enemy has the ability to cause your sickness or interfere with your healing. There are **spiritual roots** to some illness and there are **spiritual blockages** to some healings. Sometimes a person is dealing with both. Let me give you an example.

If you can only remember one thing about sickness, let it be this:

WHATEVER YOU LET INTO YOUR SOUL WILL EVENTUALLY MANIFEST IN YOUR BODY!

An individual may have arthritis because he or she has anger or resentment toward someone. This causes an over-production of a certain chemical which leads to inflammation throughout your body, especially in your joints. Spiritually speaking, when you are not "jointly fit together" with others, your joints will let you know it. This is a **spiritual root**.

On the other hand, there may or may not have been a spiritual root to the problem. If you trip and fall, I do not believe it means some demon tripped you because you had a door open in your life to the demonic. Sometimes stuff happens. But when it does, if you pray and ask God to heal it, and He doesn't, then you might get angry at God. First, this is the incorrect way to pray. Then, when you get angry, it **blocks your healing**. There might be no spiritual root to your illness, but when you don't get healed right away, you develop an offense toward the pastor who doesn't pray for you long enough, or often enough, or whatever. The issue here is to **identify the root or the blockage** and deal with it so that the healing can come.

Other things that can result in sickness are not so obvious. Breaking covenant is an open door to demonic attack. Generational curses (especially Masonic curses) can be operating behind the scenes. Doing spiritual warfare the wrong way can bring an attack. These issues are dealt with in a later chapter.

Keep in mind that the sin that is the root of your disease is not always the kind of sin you think about. The sin of adultery may eventually show up in your liver in various forms of disease, but your anger, which we don't so often think of as sin, will cause all sorts of "itis" in the body – including arthritis. Having a spirit of rejection or self-hatred will eventually cause all sorts of auto-immune diseases. Whatever you allow in your soul will eventually manifest in your body. Medical science has known about this for a long time. We, in the church, are just starting to get it now.

(4) ➤ **Rejection**. The fourth reason why people don't get saved and why people don't get healed is rejection. Rejection means that you do believe that Jesus is who He said He is, but you just don't want Him. You may even believe that Jesus died for your sins. You have faith that, if you confess Him, you'll have eternal life, but you just don't want it. There are people like that. I know some. They just don't want it. They don't want to lose control of their lives or they have some other irrational reason.

The same thing can block your healing. Now you might wonder who in his right mind would not want to be healed. Maybe some people don't want salvation, but surely everyone wants to be healed, right?

I have a friend who is an ordained minister in Russia. She told me about having a healing service in which it seemed everyone was getting healed. People were getting out of wheelchairs and throwing down their crutches and everybody was getting healed. She was going down a line of people, praying for each one. She came to a little crippled lady and started praying the prayer that was going to heal her.

The lady said, "Wait, wait, wait, wait, wait, wait, I don't want to lose my disability check. Could you just pray that the pain will go away?" She believed that she was going to be healed so much that she had to stop the minister before she healed her.

A young man in his thirties brought his mother to us for prayer. She had had a stroke, and she had cancer as well. She was dying. We dealt with many of the issues of her soul. Then we started commanding her body to be healed and thanking God. Nothing happened.

We went back to the beginning and looked for more spiritual issue that could be interfering with her healing and then we again commanded her body to be healed. Nothing happened.

I thought, "This is impossible. I know that she has to be healed. It cannot be possible that she is not healed."

So I started down my list of things that block healing. (1) Ignorance – even if she had ignorance, it did not matter because we were doing the praying, and we certainly were not ignorant. (2) Unbelief - same as number one. It did not matter if she had unbelief because we were the ones with the faith. (3) Spiritual Interference - We had dealt with all the issues God identified to us. I was only left with (4) – Rejection.

"Is it possible that she does not want healing?" I wondered.

So I asked her some questions. I asked her what her life was like before her illness. I found out that she was lonely because all her children had married and moved away.

I then asked what her life was like now that she was sick. I found out that her daughter had divorced her husband to move home with her and that her son had separated from his wife to take care of her. What would her life be like if she got healed? They would all leave her again.

It finally dawned on me that she did not want to be healed. I asked her about this. She admitted that it did not bother her to stay sick.

Jesus walked to the Pool of Bethesda. He spoke to one man there and asked him something unusual. He asked, "Do you want to be made whole?"[26]

Now that is a strange thing. I thought… "Well maybe it really means 'Do you want to be healed?'" so I looked it up. In case you have not looked it up for yourself, it doesn't mean "healed.' It means "whole"– as if there was something missing that had to be added. It comes from the root word which means "to grow or to expand." **Do you want to be made whole?** Do you want the whole package?

Let me give you the Cheryl Schang translation. Right now you are lying by the pool; somebody brings you food, and you don't have to buy your own clothes. You don't have to go to temple three times a day, you don't have to tithe, you don't have to work, and you don't have to have a job. Oh yes, you're sick, but look at the benefits!

Do you really want the whole package? Do you want to be healed if that means you have to get up and get a job and buy your own food? Do you want to take care of your own family, and go to temple three times a day, and observe all those laws and all of those rules? Do you really want the whole package – the whole thing?

There are some people who do not want the whole thing. You might think no one would reject their healing, but I am here to tell you that they will. For a variety of reasons they do not want the whole thing.

Let's look at one of the Biblical examples that falls into this category of rejecting the healing, or the package in which healing comes. This example also touches on another false teaching, so let's deal with them both here. We have told people that they need to have faith in order to get healed. One of the scriptures that we use to justify this is Matthew 13:58 where Jesus went into His hometown and He did not do many miracles there because of their unbelief. Yet we know that the crowd following Him around to see

46

the miracles was the size of a small city. There was no doubt that He could do the miracles; there was no doubt that He could heal.

The kind of unbelief Matthew speaks of in this passage is a number 4 type of road block (rejection), not a number 2 (unbelief). **It was that they rejected Him**. Notice they did not say, "We are not certain that He can really heal." Notice what they did say: "Who is this? Isn't this Joseph and Mary's son? Who does He think He is?"

I will release a new book soon, on how to do signs and wonders for unbelievers. In it I will discuss the fact that Jesus was performing what were considered the miracles of the Messiah, and they rejected him on that basis. They had unbelief that He was the Messiah. They did not have unbelief (lack of faith) in His ability to heal.

So, let us review. These four things can block your salvation: ignorance, unbelief, spiritual interference, and rejection. They are the same four things that block your healing, because healing and salvation are in the same package.

Here is the question that you are probably asking yourself now: "Well, if I'm not healed, am I saved?" Isn't that the next logical question?

Remember, I just told you they were in the same package. They can't be separated. Let me answer your question.

The word for salvation in the Greek is *sozo*. I want to give you the definition of *sozo* from a couple of good sources.

Salvation - sozo: means everything that God can do for us. This includes eternal life, but it is more than simply the new birth experience.

> ➤ Strong's – deliver or protect (lit or fig), to heal, to preserve, to save yourself, to do well, to be made whole

➤ Septuagint– to save, to keep safe and sound, to rescue from danger or destruction, to save one who is suffering from disease or is perishing, to make well, to heal, to restore to health, to include spiritual healing, to rescue, to bring safely forth from, to save in a technical Biblical sense, to deliver from the penalties of Messianic judgment, to save from the evils which are an obstruction of the Messianic deliverance, to make one a partner to the salvation of Christ.

➤ Vine's Complete Expository Dictionary – the material and temporal deliverance from dangerous sufferings, of the spiritual and eternal salvations granted immediately by God to those who believe in the Lord Jesus Christ, the present experiences of God's power to deliver from the bondage of sin, the future deliverance of believers at the second coming of Christ, inclusively for all the blessings bestowed by God on man in Christ.

So the question then is this: if that is salvation, if that is the whole package, what are we missing?

First I would like to make the distinction between "salvation" and being "born again" since they are different words in the Greek.

We see the concept of being "born again" in John 3:16 – *"Whosoever believes in Him will not perish but will have eternal life."* This term for eternal life is *aionios zoe* (perpetual life). If you believe, you are born again and you get eternal life. We are justified by faith; it is instant, it is miraculous. It is John 3:16 – it is eternal life. It happens instantaneously, and there is nothing you can do to earn it or deserve it. It is a free gift.

Once you are justified by faith, and you have eternal

Phil,
2 1/2

life, you begin the process of sanctification. The scriptures tell us to work out our salvation with fear and trembling.[27] Have you ever wondered about that? How can you work out your salvation, if salvation is a free gift? You can't earn your salvation. You do not receive salvation by works. So how can you work out your salvation with fear and trembling? Here is how.

We have the word "salvation" mixed up with eternal life, which is the result of being "born again." Justification comes by the grace of God. But our processing does not stop there. Once He has given us eternal life, He begins to clean us up. This is *sozo*; getting the whole package. This is the sanctification process.

Your healing is in the *sozo*. You are entitled to it because you have been justified. It's your inheritance. You deserve it, and if you don't have it, you are being robbed. Your healing is in your *sozo*.

You must fight for it, because it belongs to you. The enemy would like to rob you by convincing you that it does not belong to you. Just like one who has inherited a fortune, if you let a dishonest trustee tell you that it is not yours, you can be cheated out of what belongs to you.

The same is true of your healing. This explains how you can walk around not healed and yet you are born again. You are even now in the process of working out your *sozo* - which includes your healing. Never again wonder if God wants you to be healed. It is in your package, you are entitled to it, and you work it out until you have it. Don't be denied.

Healing is in your *sozo*. You read it earlier but did you catch it? Let me give you a good scriptural example that you will all recognize. Remember the woman with the issue of blood? She said, "If I may but touch His garment, I shall be whole."[28] The word "whole" is *sozo*. In the account given in Mark, we read that immediately her blood flow stopped and she was healed of the plague.

Very clearly we see that physical healing is included in your *sozo*. It is an integral, inseparable part of your salvation. It is part of being returned to the condition of wholeness.

[14] McCrossen, 25

[15] 1 John 3:8

[16] McCrossen, 23-24. "Again we are very sure that the 'our' of Isaiah 53:4 and Matthew 8:17 includes us today, because of the way Matthew expresses himself in the Greek: 'Himself took our infirmities.' 'Our infirmities' reads in Greek, *tas astheneias hemon* (the sicknesses of us). This is consistent with 1 Corinthians 15:3 'Christ died for our sins.' 'For our sins' reads in the Greek *uper ton hamartion hemon* (for the sins of us). The same word is used in 1 Peter 2:24. The word 'our' is *hemon*. 'Who his own self bare our sins in his own body on the tree.' 'Our sins' here reads in the *Greek tas hamartias hemon* (the sins of us)."

[17] 2 Peter 3:9,and Matthew 18:14

[18] Acts 10:38

[19] Mark 3:24

[20] James 3:11

[21] Romans 8:11

[22] John 10:10

[23] Mark 2:10-11

[24] 2 Corinthians 4:4

[25] John 8:32

[26] John 5:6

[27] Philippians 2:12

[28] Matthew 9:21 and Mark 5:28

Section 2

The Role of Faith

Got Faith?

If you already had the kind of faith that you needed to be healed, or if you knew how and when to use that faith, you probably would not be reading this book. Let's assume that you are a bit short in the faith department. Or maybe you just think you are short of faith.

One of the most important discoveries I have made as I studied healing is that we have used faith inappropriately. When this inappropriate use of faith did not produce the results, we all figured we just did not have enough faith, or that God did not really intend for all to be healed, or we held some other equally wrong idea.

Here is what I mean by an inappropriate use of faith. In the past, many of us were taught that if we just believed hard enough... long enough... passionately enough, then we would be healed. I don't have to tell most of you that it does not work this way. Remember the four things that block salvation/healing? If your only problem is number 2 – unbelief – then this kind of faith will work.

This is not the case with most believers who have been sick for a prolonged time. Most of the time, when believers have a prolonged illness, the blockage is a number 3 type – spiritual interference. Until you remove the spiritual root, or the spiritual blockage, all the faith you have will not work. **You must first remove the blockage and then use your faith**. When you do it this way, it really takes very little faith to bring about the healing.

In a later chapter, I will talk about how to get someone healed who does not have his or her own faith. In this section, I want to help you get your own faith so that you are not a victim of the enemy. Are you convinced yet that healing belongs to you? If so, then half the faith battle is won.

Where is your faith? Your faith is not in the cognitive processes of your head. It doesn't exist there; it can't be birthed there. If you are trying to get it there, good luck. Faith is in your heart. Here are four scriptures to prove it.

Mark 11:23...do not doubt in your heart.
Luke 24:25... you are slow of heart to believe.
Acts 8:37...if you believe with all your heart.
Romans 10:9...believe in your heart.

Where's your faith? It is in your heart. So, you fill your heart up with the word of God, the *logos* word. This word then becomes the foundation of your faith. Then your faith has something with which to work.

Luke 8:12 says that the devil comes to take away the word from your heart so you might not believe and be saved (*sozo*). If the devil can steal something from your heart (where it is supposed to produce faith), then you he can rob you of your *sozo*. But if you have faith in your heart, then it can produce your *sozo*.

God's word is medicine to your flesh.[29] I had a professor in seminary who started out life as a farmer. He went to college in Texas to learn agriculture. During that time, as part of his curriculum, he had to take two semesters of animal husbandry.

For these courses, the students had to study sheep, and he complained about this. "Why do I have to study sheep? I am going to be a farmer. I never want anything to do with sheep; I don't need to know about sheep."

But he said, looking back, that he learned more in that class on how to be a pastor than he did in seminary. He said, "Did you know that a sheep has, as part of its body, the capability to heal itself of every single disease that a sheep can get?"

Do you think that's one of the reasons why God called us sheep?

However, there is a catch; you've got to keep the sheep eating. If the sheep stops eating, it will die. Naturally, the first thing a sheep wants to do when it gets sick is to stop eating.

We are supposed to take the Word of God like medicine, like we are eating it. The Word of God is medicine to your flesh. What is the first thing that we do when we get sick? We stop reading the Word. We don't feel like being spiritual when we are sick.

Or you may think that the word is not working because you got sick in the first place. Wrong! That is a lie of the enemy designed to rob you of your healing.

This professor, who was also a pastor of a church here in my city, had a way of dealing with sick people. When someone in his congregation called him to tell him they were sick or in pain, he would say, "I have a scripture for you." Then he would open the Bible and give them a chapter to read. He would tell them to meditate on that chapter and let him know what God told them.

A week or two later and he would see the person and ask about their ailment. They would say, "It is fine, but let me tell you what God showed me on that scripture you gave me." **He kept them eating.** The word is medicine to your flesh. So if you are sick, don't stop eating. The word goes in and it produces faith, and it will lead you to your *sozo.*

If you don't have faith, the Bible gives you three ways to get faith. Memorize them; you never know when you will need them.

➤ Prayer and Fasting

The first one is found in a scripture that we examined earlier – Matthew 17. The disciples came to Jesus and asked why they couldn't cast out the demon. He told them it was because of their unbelief, "*...this kind goes out by prayer and fasting.*" **He diagnosed the problem as unbelief and he prescribed the remedy as prayer and fasting.** When you need some faith, pray and fast. That is the hard one. I will tell you an easier one.

➤ Pray in the Spirit

Jude 20 says, "*...building up yourself on your most holy faith, praying in the Holy Ghost.*" This one really works. This is praying in tongues; using your prayer language.

Let me give you a tip. If you are using this scripture to get faith, don't pray in tongues quietly and softly. When you are praying in the spirit, you are actually declaring the will of God on the earth, so you should speak in tongues the same way you would speak to disease and sickness. Pray in tongues loudly – so loudly that you drown out those lying thoughts that tell you this won't work. Do that for twenty minutes, and you will feel ten feet tall. You will just wish there was a demon standing near by so that you could bite its head off!

> ## ➢ Get a *Rhema* Word

The third way you get faith it is to get a *rhema* word. Romans 10:17 states that *"...faith comes by hearing and hearing by the word of God."*

The word "word" in this passage of Scripture is not *logos.* It is *rhema.* If you have been in the company of believers very long, you have probably been exposed to the distinction. *Logos* is generally used to refer to the written Word of God and *rhema* is generally used to refer to the uttered, current word of God, or what we have come to call a prophetic word. So, if you need some faith, get yourself a *rhema.* It's not hard. Pray (in tongues), then get quite and listen. You will hear God speak. He tells you what to do to get your healing, and faith is instantly born in you.

If you really need a lot of faith, do all three. That is what I usually do before I go to minister healing to someone.

Now that you have faith, what do you do with it? Faith speaks. Faith has a voice. Matthew 12:34 says *"...out of the abundance of your heart..."* (What is located in your heart? Your faith.) *"...out of the abundance of your heart the mouth speaks."* Luke 6:45 says:

> *"a good man out of the good treasure of his heart brings forth good; and an evil man out of the evil treasure of his heart brings forth evil. For of the abundance of the heart his mouth speaks."* (NKJV)

Faith is not just a tool; faith is the evidence. Hebrews 11:1 tells us that faith is both substance and evidence. If you are a lawyer, maybe you are familiar with the legal definition of the word evidence. For the rest of us, here it is:

Evidence means the documentary or oral statements and the material objects admissible as testimony in a court of law. According to the scripture, that is also the definition of faith, because faith IS the evidence. *"Faith is the substance of things hoped for, (faith is) the evidence of things not seen."* Said another way, faith is proof. It is tangible documentary proof; proof that is admissible in a court of law.

God is into legal. I am thankful He is not into legalism, but God is into legal. He is into legal because He is a just God and by His laws we have justice. Sometimes He talks to us in legal terms.

The whole Covenant is all about who God is and how He works with man; what His obligations are, and what ours are. There were over six hundred laws in the Old Covenant. God wanted to make sure that all the terms and conditions were well understood. But God said something amazing in Psalms. He said, *"I have magnified my word above my name."*[30]

It is a remarkable verse, and I can't even tell you that I have the whole revelation of it yet. However, here is what I do have: in this verse God makes a monumental commitment. The limitless, boundless, infinite God chooses to limit Himself!

One of the names of God is Omnipotent. God is All Powerful! He can do anything. He is sovereign. But this God, who can do anything, limited Himself to His word, that we might know Him. He was saying, "I have magnified My word above My name and so, although I can, I won't, because I wrote it down so you could know me. I did it so that you could have justice, so you could count on me, so that you could know what was in your contract."

Have you heard people say that God might not want to heal everybody, because God is sovereign? Yes He is sovereign, but He decided to limit His sovereignty to His word. His Word-Made-Flesh (Jesus) proved, by His action, that you may all (everybody, whosoever, whatsoever, totally, thoroughly, wholly, completely) be healed. God put in His word that we could, *"lay hands on the sick and they will recover."*[31]

Because He said it, and because He wrote it down, it is now magnified above His sovereign name. Amazing! We now have the evidence written right here in our contract – the Bible. It is in the contract that you are entitled to be healed. Because you are born again, you are entitled to the full *sozo* package. You don't have to wonder if God is going heal you. You don't have to wonder if it is in His sovereign will. He has already written it down, and even if He wanted to change His mind, He can't. He has put it in writing and that means He is committed to it. He has magnified His word (by his stripes you are healed) above His sovereign name.

It is not enough to just have faith. You must use faith. Faith is an act. Everything you get from God, you get by using faith. How did you get saved? *"By grace you are saved through faith."*[32] Everything you get from God, you have to get by faith.

Faith is the coin of the realm of heaven. If you want to buy something here in America, you must use American dollars. If you go to London, you need to use pounds, and if you go to Germany, you have to use euros. If you want something from God, you have to use your faith because it is the only way to obtain things in the spirit realm. It is the coin of the spirit realm. Once you have it, you can use it to get your own healing. So once you get faith, here is how you use it – believe and speak.

In my New Testament seminary course, I started off with an attitude. The professor started his lecture at such an elementary level, I thought I would die of boredom before the break. He started his lecture by saying that all things mentioned in the New Testament fall into one of two categories.

"The first category is a promise. A promise is something that has not been fulfilled. The second thing is a fact. Facts are promises that have already been fulfilled. "

By this time, I was wondering if there was any way to get out of this course. He went on…..

"Now, you would never ask for a fact to be fulfilled because a fact is already fulfilled. It's the promise that needs to be fulfilled. "

I was looking at my watch, thinking of all the things I could have been doing instead of listening to "kindergarten Bible school." He went on…

"If you were praying for a fact to be fulfilled, it would be like praying, 'Oh God would you please send the Messiah, and let Him be born of a virgin, in the town of Bethlehem.' Would we ever pray that?"

Then it dawned on me……Oh wait a minute – I have been asking for a fact to be fulfilled when I was praying for healing. I had prayed, "God, would you please heal Linda?" That is the same thing as praying, "Oh God, would you send Messiah and let Him be born of a virgin in Bethlehem?" **I had been treating a fact like it was a promise.**
Your healing was paid for in full 2000 years ago at the cross of Calvary, and you don't have to ask God if He will do it for you. We don't have to pray, "If it be your will to heal…" He has already made His will known.
All of the sudden the Lord brought back to my mind a conversation He had with me months earlier. I didn't "get it" back then, but it all made sense as this professor was speaking.

I had been praying for my friend, who was quite ill. I opened my mouth to pray and ask God to heal my friend, but before I could get a word out, God spoke to me. He asked me, "What are you going to ask me to do that I have not already done?"

I almost choked on the words I was about to pray. I was left speechless. I could not figure out what to pray at that point.

Now, as the professor spoke, I suddenly understood what God had been saying to me. I was about to ask him to fulfill a fact. Healing was promised, as Isaiah the prophet had said. The promise was fulfilled at Calvary. Later, Peter spoke of it in the past tense. It was an accomplished fact.

There was nothing more for God to do; He had done His part. There was nothing more for Jesus to do; He had done His part. The only one who had not done their part was me.

I saw our duty in terms of a military occupation force. The Captain of the Hosts had come, fought, and won the battle. The victory belonged to the conquering King. He then left the battlefield to return to headquarters, and he left an occupation army (us) in the land. He told us to "occupy till I come."[33] We are simply in charge of enforcing the victory. We do not have to re-fight or re-win the battle. **We only have to enforce what has already been done.**

We are not to pray and ask God to heal.
We are to command the healing that was purchased.

It is almost impossible to use your faith if you think you have to get God to do something that He may not want to do. It is easy to use your faith if you realize that all you must do is use your words to enforce what God has already done.

When you use your faith to enforce your rights, you are not operating in presumption. It does not offend God. Presumption is when you assume you know what God wants without even bothering to find out what He really wants.

The Bible makes it absolutely clear that God wants you healed – here – in this lifetime. It is, therefore, not presumption to enforce the known will of God on the earth. If anything, it is presumption **not** to get someone healed.

I will say it again. You get what is yours by using your faith. Faith speaks. Thanks to Rev. Kenneth Hagin, the great faith teacher, many believers can quote Mark 11:23 by heart. Jesus said,

> *"For surely I **say** unto you, That whosoever shall **say** unto this mountain, Be thou removed, and be thou cast into the sea; and shall not doubt in his heart, but shall believe that those things which he **says** shall come to pass; he shall have whatsoever he **says**."*

The word "say" or "says" is used four times in that verse. The word "believe" is only used once. That tells me that it takes a little bit of believing and a whole lot of saying.

> ➤ The first "say" is the Greek word *lego.* What does that bring to mind? Lego building blocks? That is exactly what you should think of because that Greek word means "a set, systematic discourse." If you were building a house, it would be like an architect framing up the house: putting the framework, the building blocks in place.
> ➤ The next time you see that word "say," it is the Greek word, *epo*, which means to command.
> ➤ The third time you see that word, it's the Greek word *laleo,* which means to speak with a loud voice.

➤ And the last time you see that word, it is *lego* again.

So here is the picture Jesus was painting about how to move mountains with your faith: Do you want to frame up your world? Command it, speak it with a loud voice, and by that voice of faith you will frame your world.

You don't like your life? Look at what you are saying. I am serious. **You are "framed" by your words.** So when your faith speaks, you need the right words to frame your victory. Speak the *logos,* speak the *rhema.*

There is already power in those words. If God has spoken them, then power was released. That power that was present when He first spoke those words is contained in the words, even now. **The word of the Lord never loses its power.** Get yourself a *rhema* or speak the *logos.*

God spoke and created the worlds. He said, *"Let there be light,"* and there was light. We still have that light. The words that God spoke thousands of years ago are still working. So there must still be power in those words. **When God speaks, the power lives forever.** If He spoke it once, it is still alive, and it still has power in it. Pick it up and plug it in.

Hebrews 4:2 tells us that the word that was preached did not profit them because it was not mixed with faith. I learned something from Rev. Kenneth Hagin. He said that when he prays for people, he never knows whether it's going to be a miracle, which is instant, or whether it's going to be a healing, which is a process.

We're not guaranteed the miracle but we are guaranteed the healing. Some people get a miracle, but you can't always count on it. But you can absolutely go to the bank with the promise of healing, which is the process of your body healing itself or recovering. When God is involved in the healing process, it is usually much quicker than anything we could imagine.

Kenneth Hagin laid hands on people and prayed for them. Sometimes a miracle happened and sometimes the recovery started. He gave them this instruction: "Go home tonight and get in bed and say, 'Thank You God, that your power went into my body tonight and it is working now to effect a healing and a cure." When you get up tomorrow morning say, "Thank You God that your healing power is working in my body right now, and I will see the cure." When you pray over your food at noon, bow your head and say, "Thank You God that healing power came into my body, and it is working even now to bring a total healing and a cure."

He told story after story of people whose healing manifested as they were thanking God.[34] He told the story of how one person left his meeting still in a wheelchair. For three days that man thanked God that the healing power was working in his body to bring a full recovery. On the third day the man just got up out of his wheelchair and walked.

Your faith must speak. It must agree with the Word of God. Dig in your heals, and don't let go. Grab hold of that word by faith. Don't stop speaking it.

I have heard members of the faith movement discuss the conflict they feel declaring they are healed before the healing manifested. Is it faith or is it a lie?

I never tell people to walk around saying they are healed before they see the manifestation of it. If they have not removed all the roots or blockages, then they are not healed. What they can say truthfully, and still have the words be full of faith, is this: God's healing power is working in my body to bring a full recovery.

Just saying, "I am healed," without dealing with the blockage will produce NO results. Once you remove the hindrances to healing and release the power of the Holy Spirit on that flesh, something will happen. **Use your faith AFTER you remove the blockage.**

Rev. Norville Hayes tells a wonderful story about

declaring healing. His daughter's body was covered with warts. She had forty-two of them. She was approximately fifteen years old, and you know how embarrassing that would be for a fifteen year old girl. Rev. Kenneth Hagin was traveling through their town, and he called the Hayes family and invited himself to stay at their house.

Shortly after he arrived, the daughter said to Pastor Hagin, "Please talk to my daddy about letting the doctor cut off these warts."

She had had them cut off one time before, and they had all come back, plus more. For this reason, Pastor Hayes wasn't really excited about the idea of having them cut off again.

Pastor Hagin said, "Oh honey, I can curse those warts and they'll die."

I learned from others who minister in healing that when you have cancer, tumors, growths and warts, you curse them. They are cells in rebellion, and you treat them just like Jesus did the fig tree. If you are dealing with any of these physical symptoms, check up to see if there is any rebellion in your life. Whatever you let in your soul will eventually manifest in your body.

Back to the story... Pastor Hagin said, "Honey I can curse those warts and they'll die," and everybody looked at him like he was nuts.

Curse warts and they'll die? Now, we know from Scripture that when **Jesus** cursed something it died, don't we?

Before they had a chance to actually curse the warts, Pastor Hagin got a phone call and he had to leave. A couple of days later Pastor Hayes was walking through the living room and his daughter was sitting there with her boyfriend. As he passed them, he heard the Lord say, "How long are you going to let those warts stay on your daughter's body?"

He thought, "Well, not another minute, I guess." He

thought… "My daughter is going to kill me"…but he walked into the room and said, "I curse those warts in the name of Jesus! Wither up and die!" Then he turned and walked out.

The daughter was mortified. "Oh Daddy, you embarrassed me so much…."

From that moment on Pastor Hayes started saying, "I thank You, God, that those warts are disappearing from my daughter's body; I thank You, God, that they are withering up and dying even now." He said it morning, noon and night.

Finally, after two weeks, the daughter confronted him. She was in tears: "Just STOP! I can't stand it! I wake up in the morning and I hear you saying, 'Thank you, God, for taking those warts off my daughter.' I go to bed at night and I hear you saying, 'Thank you, God, for removing those warts from my daughter's body.'" She said, "I have forty-two warts, I've always had forty-two warts. I count them every single morning. I still have every one of those forty-two warts. I can't stand hearing you pray this anymore!"

So, what do you think Pastor Hayes did? **He increased his thanksgiving to hurry up the results!** Every single time that the thought came into his head he said, "Thank You, God, that you are removing those warts from my daughter's body. Thank You that they are going away, for they are cursed and they cannot live in her body, I praise your name."

One week later the daughter came home from school and she said, "Daddy, can I ask you a question? Every morning I get up and I count my warts. I have forty-two warts, and it's always the same. This morning, when I got up and counted, I had thirty-four. Where did the other eight go?"

He said, "I don't know, but the other thirty-four are going there as well!" He stepped it up another notch.

One week later she was hanging clothes up in her closet. You know how teenagers can get this big mess of clothes at the bottom of the closet? She was hanging up dresses. As she was hanging them up she was looking at her hand. In the middle of this chore, she looked at her hand and all the warts were suddenly gone. All, totally gone, permanently! They've never come back. First, you see, he dealt with the work of the enemy; then he released his faith. That is what it's like to get your *sozo*. **Don't be denied.** And did you notice in the story that the daughter seemed to have no faith for her own healing?

A few years ago my dog was diagnosed with cancer, cutaneous carcinoma, a type of skin cancer… lumps under the skin. It was covering her body—she was absolutely covered! I took her to the vet and they said it was skin cancer. They offered to treat it with radiation. I took her to another vet and they biopsied one of the lumps. They examined it under the microscope and they announced, "Yes, it is absolutely cancer."

We did not want to give her radiation treatments. She was an eleven-year-old dog. I thought, "Okay, I will just pray over her."

So my dog, **who had no faith**, started getting daily prayer. I put her up on the bed with me every morning and, for about five minutes, I would put my hand upon her head and speak over her. I had to find a verse.

I had to have a *logos*, a *rhema,* or something in which to put my faith. I knew that my dog was not covered by the sacrifice of Jesus. Healing was not in the atonement for her, so I needed something else. I found something I could use in Deuteronomy 28 where the Lord promised to bless both the land and the herds for His people's sake.

"Miss Pepper, you are my herd, and I bless you in the name of the Lord. I say that I am in covenant with Jehovah God and He will deny me no good thing. You are my herd and you are blessed and you are prosperous. Cancer will not cross the threshold of my door; I rebuke it in the name of Jesus. I curse these lumps, I curse this cancer, and I declare that you are whole and you are healed!"

I did that maybe five minutes a day, and I did it almost everyday. Sometimes I traveled and I could not do it.

Thirty days later, everything looked exactly the same; there was no change. I kept it up, and after sixty days I noticed that she had fewer lumps. I was not really sure at first. I kept asking people, "Does my dog look like she has fewer lumps to you? I think that she has fewer lumps."

I kept it up and, at the end of ninety days, there was not a lump left in her body. I took her to the vet and the vet said that the dog had no trace of cancer. Let me again point out the obvious: **my dog had no faith.**

If I had known then what I know now, I would have been doing it ten times a day and it wouldn't have taken me ninety days. But this is how long it took me with prayer just five minutes a day. I hope it doesn't take you that long. That's what it means to get your full package. That's what it takes. Do not be denied; don't let Satan steal your stuff.

In addition to saying the right thing, you need to make sure that you don't say the WRONG thing! You need to guard your tongue. Jesus promised us (or warned us) that you will have whatsoever you say.[35] **YOU WILL HAVE WHATSOEVER YOU SAY!** King David said, *"Set a watch, oh Lord, before my mouth. Keep the door of my lips."*[36] Let me give you a picture to carry around in your mind about what "set a watch" means.

I heard a preacher tell the story of a minister who went to Soviet Russia. He had to go to a bank to change money. He found the bank, but the door was locked. He knocked on the door. A guard with an Uzi gun came to the door and demanded, "What do you want?"

The minister said that he needed to get money. The guard opened the door and stepped out onto the street. He looked one way, then the other way. He looked at the minister and said, "Okay, come on in."

The whole time, the guard kept his gun pointed at the minister. The minister told how he was almost afraid to move. The whole time he was there getting money, he had an Uzi pointed at him. When he left, the guard followed him, opened the door, looked out, let him out, then locked the door.

That doesn't sound like our kind of bank guard does it? Our bank guards are much more relaxed and friendly. We don't really think of their job as defending the bank. They could probably give you a description of who robbed the place!

Don't get me wrong, sometimes it's important to know who robbed you. But I suspect when David asked the Lord to put a guard on his mouth, he was talking about the kind of guard with an Uzi gun.

Here is what you need to do. The next time a word that is not full of faith, or that is full of negative faith, wants to get in, stop it at the door. Say, "What business do you have in my mouth? What are you trying to accomplish? No, you are not getting in here, because the last time I let you in here, you robbed me of everything I had. You're not getting in my mouth." That's what putting a guard on your mouth means to me. *"I will take heed to my ways that I sin not with my tongue; I will keep my mouth with a bridle."* [37] *Ps 39:1*

I know of a preacher from Louisiana whose elders invited him to go coyote hunting. He wasn't all that keen about hunting coyotes, but he thought … "I get to dress up like Rambo so I'll give it a try."

He got out in the woods and some of the guys had a coyote call. A coyote call is like a duck call, which makes a noise that attracts the ducks. They had a coyote call that made a sound that attracts coyotes. Do you know what the coyote call sounded like? It made the sound of a wounded rabbit. In that instant the Lord spoke to him and said, "When we whine, we attract the enemy."

Just like the coyote is attracted to a wounded rabbit, so are demons attracted to whiners. Sniff, sniff, sniff, LUNCH! Easy prey. **Don't whine if don't want every demon in your neighborhood sniffing you out and thinking you're lunch.** Sometimes we need to bind our mouths more than we need to bind the devil. We have been robbed by our own mouths.

Dr. Yung E. Cho has a large church in Seoul, Korea. Pastor Mark Hankins tells the story about Dr. Cho having lunch with the top neurosurgeon in Korea. This neurosurgeon said to him, "Cho, we've made an amazing new discovery. We have discovered that the speech center of the brain controls the whole central nervous system. You know we can touch one area in the brain and the arm will move, and we can touch another area in the brain and the leg will move but, if we touch the speech center, the entire central nervous system responds. So much so that, if a person says, 'I am weak,' the entire body begins to prepare to be weak."

Cho said, "I knew that."

The neurosurgeon said, "You couldn't know this because it is the latest discovery. This is the latest thing. We just found it out. How did you know?"

Cho said, "Dr. James 3:5, tongue is tiny member, controls the whole body."

There is actually something physical that happens in your body when you speak. God built it into you, and when you confess doubt and unbelief, sickness and disease, your body prepares to make that happen. When you confess faith, health and healing and declare who God is, and what He has done, and what belongs to you, your body begins to prepare to receive that. You make it happen with your words. **Once you remove the blockage, your body will respond to faith filled words of health.**

The apostle James tells us the tongue is like the rudder on a ship. The translation from the Message Bible reads:

"If you could find someone whose speech is perfectly true, you would have a perfect person in perfect control of their lives. A bit in the mouth of a horse controls the whole horse. A small rudder on a huge ship in the hands of a skilled captain sets the course in the face of the strongest wind. A word out of your mouth may seem of no account, but it can accomplish nearly anything or destroy it."[38]

If you are old enough, you may remember the Cuban missile crisis. America didn't want the Russians to get any weapons to Cuba, so we circled the island with our ships to embargo it. Our troops were given instructions that, if Russian ships approached, they were to fire two shots. The first shot was over the bow and was a warning shot. If the Russian ships didn't turn back, then the second shot was to take out their rudder.

This is the same plan that Satan uses. He will fire a warning shot to make you scared. If you don't back off, he will aim for your rudder, which is your mouth. If he can take out your mouth, he's got you, because **your victory is in your own mouth**.

---

[29] Proverbs 4:20-22

[30] Psalms 138:2

[31] Mark 16:18

[32] Ephesians 2:8

[33] Luke 19:13

[34] Hagin, Kenneth E., "The Healing Anointing", Rhema Bible Church, Tulsa, OK, 1997.

[35] Mark 11:23

[36] Psalms 141:3

[37] Psalms 39:1

[38] James 3:4

The Prayer of Faith

If you are going to pray for others to be healed, you need to have enough faith for them. They may not have any of their own.

Faith is a belief, not a hope. You can only have faith if there is no lingering doubt. If you have doubt, you don't have faith, you have hope. This presents a problem for most of us who often have a bit of doubt. I will give you ways to pray prayers of faith that overcome this problem.

Faith is belief that does not rest on logical proof or material evidence.

I build my faith when I get a *rhema* word from God, or when I read a promise in His word. For me, it is impossible to have faith unless I hear God speak, or unless I have read the Word.

When you think about it, we have built our entire Christian religion on faith – that is a belief that does not rest on logical proof or material evidence. We believe we have eternal life and we will live with the Lord in heaven, simply because we read it in the Word. We have no other tangible proof. Yet we live our lives as though we had a contract in our desk drawer deeding us a piece of land in heaven. The same kind of faith is used to bring the manifestation of healing. All the faith you need is the same amount you have for your salvation.

Each time I look at the sick person for whom I am about to pray, I have faith. I will tell you one of my secrets. I cannot say that I immediately have faith that they will be healed. I build up to it. First, I have faith that God is faithful to His Word. Then I have faith that I know His word tells me that He wants EVERYONE healed. Then I have faith that I can hear Him tell me what is blocking the healing. Then I have faith that if I remove the blockage, the body will recovery. In other words, I have faith in Him and the process, and that leads me to faith in the outcome. I hope you see the difference.

Now, if you really believe that God's word concerning healing is true, what kind of prayer is there left to pray? Do you believe that because God said it, it is an accomplished fact? The only thing left to do when someone has bought you an expensive gift is to say thank you. The prayer of faith can best be summed up in these words: **Thank you.**

Thanks is always connected to belief, the understanding and the trust that you have been given something. The prayer of faith is, "Thank You, Father, that I have the thing that you told me I am going to get." He gave you healing; it is written down in your contract. The prayer of faith must include a "Thank You."

There is power in this truth. When Jesus needed a miracle, this is how He accomplished it. When He had to feed five thousand people with a sack lunch, He prayed "Thank you!"

One of His biggest miracles was raising Lazarus from the dead. He stood in front of the tomb of Lazarus, who had been dead four days. What did He do? He turned His face towards heaven and He said, "Thank You, Father, that you've heard me." When Jesus needed a miracle, He prayed a prayer of faith.

Part of our failure in the area of faith has been the wrong

timing of the prayer of faith. We have been taught that if we just had enough faith, we could be healed. **This is a lie!**

There is more to it than that. Remember, sometimes Jesus had to cast out a demon in order to "heal" someone. The woman who was bent over for 18 years did not have osteoporosis or scoliosis.[39] She had a spirit of infirmity. Jesus had to kick out that spirit of infirmity in order to heal her. Jesus had tons of faith, but His faith alone was not the only tool needed. He had to remove the culprit before His faith was of any use.

Many of us were taught to use our faith before we had dealt with the blockage. This inappropriate use of faith produced NO results and we threw away the whole healing ministry. Yet, the only problem was that we used our faith out of order.

I have seen people die while using all their faith to believe God for the healing. There was a woman in my circle of friends that got cancer. She was a good, godly woman. We prayed and fasted, and prayed and fasted. Nothing changed. One day a team of women went to pray for her. As they were praying, one of the women got a *rhema* word that the lady with cancer had unforgiveness in her heart toward someone. The lady admitted that was correct, and said she would never forgive the offender. That lady died, believing to her last breath that God would heal her, but refusing to deal with the blockage.

Once we remove the thing that is blocking the healing, it only takes a tiny amount of faith to bring the results. The Bible tells us that all we need is faith the size of a mustard seed.[40] That is a tiny, tiny amount. There have been times when I had very little faith for someone, but they were healed anyway. It does not take very much faith when the faith is used at the right time.

Let my share the story of my starting place. When I was first learning to use my faith for healing, I was not sure how

I could really believe that God was going to heal everyone. I had seen prayers for the sick fail so much in the past. I had to find a place of faith, and I found it in the Lord Himself. I starting praying this way:

> "God, I have faith in your faithfulness. When all else fails me, You never will. You are the very definition of faithfulness. I would not even understand what the word "faithful" meant if I did not have Your example of faithfulness. You are faithful to Your word, Lord. Because Your word says that healing was purchased for us on Calvary, I believe it. I do not believe it for any other reason, other than because You said it."

This may not sound as strong as some of the faith-filled prayers you have heard, but it was enough. I can now pray with greater assurance than this, because I have seen person after person healed from incurable diseases or traumas. But just this little bit of pure faith was enough to get many people healed.

---

[39] Luke 13:11

[40] Luke 17:6

Use Someone Else's Faith

"Is any sick among you? let him call for the elders of the church; and let them pray over him, anointing him with oil in the name of the Lord: and the prayer of faith shall save the sick, and the Lord shall raise him up; and if he have committed sins, they shall be forgiven him. Confess your faults one to another, and pray one for another, that ye may be healed. The effectual fervent prayer of a righteous man availeth much."[41] ~James

These three verses are loaded with revelation. Let's take them piece by piece to see what treasures we have let lay in the dust.

These words were written to the believers. Based on the way this passage begins, it is almost as if James were saying, "If you are still sick, you must not have your own faith."

It is no stretch of the imagination to think that God wants us healed so much that, if we do not have our own faith, He will let us use someone else's faith. I will prove this through the scriptures in the next few pages.

This passage in James reminds us of the lesson we

learned in Matthew 17. To refresh your memory, Jesus told the disciples that they were supposed to be the ones with the faith. In this passage in James, we are once again told that **the ministers are to be the ones with the faith, not necessarily the sick person.** The elders are to exercise their faith. If you follow James' instructions to the believers, you will be healed even if you don't have any faith of your own. It is hard to have faith when you are sick and hurting.

While reading this scripture, I became curious about the oil. It says that the elders will anoint you with oil. I have a friend who makes anointing oil. I called him and asked, "What's the deal with the oil? Is it something special? Are you supposed to say something special? Does it have some special power, or what?"

He said, "In Biblical times every god had his own anointing oil. And every god had a special formula for anointing oil. Jehovah God also had a special formula for His anointing oil.[42] He forbade anyone to duplicate His formula for anointing oil.[43] **So when you put anointing oil on someone, you are marking them with the mark of that god.** This was very common in all people groups of Old Testament times.

And so our God was saying, "I have my own oil, and, when you mark somebody with that oil, you are marking them with the mark of Jehovah God, and I am obligated to them because they wear My mark; and they will be healed."

You pray the prayer of faith – they are God's, they are marked. Healing belongs to the believer.

Notice that the oil was not the only tool. It was to be combined with the prayer of faith – not the faith of the sick person, but the faith of the elders. This is another clear proof that the sick person does not have to be the one with the faith.

I had an opportunity to test this fact myself on a woman who had no faith of her own. I was teaching a healing course in a West Coast city. There was a girl there who was raised in a denomination that does not believe in healing, but she came to the class because a friend invited her. This girl was excited by what she saw and heard in the seminar. People were getting healed in the meetings. She asked if she could bring her mother, who had fibromyalgia. She warned me that her mother did not believe in healing. I told her that it did not matter; I always expect to be the one with the faith.

The next night her parents came. This was a practice night for the students, and a large group of them gathered around her to practice what they had learned. I asked this woman if we could pray for her, and she agreed. She said that she had never prayed for herself for healing, nor had she had anyone else pray for her. She told us she did not believe she would be healed.

I told her that was fine, that she would still be healed because we were not going to use her faith; we would use our faith. We began to pray for a word of knowledge. (I will tell you more about the word of knowledge later, since this is how we start the healing process.)

The woman was in extreme pain. She could hardly move her body. As we prayed, I saw her as a young woman in her late teens and I saw that someone had done something bad to her. One student said that she saw a hand and I understood this to mean that she thought that the bad thing was the work of her own hand.

I spoke gently to the woman and said that when she was a young woman of about 17 years old, there had been something bad that happened to her, and she always thought that it was her own fault.

The woman started crying. She admitted that this was true and she had never told anyone. She had kept the pain inside all these years. **Remember, whatever you let rule your soul will eventually rule your body.**

I prophesied over her that the Lord said that it was not her fault. We commanded the spirit of guilt and pain to get out, and then we commanded her body to be healed. Within a short time, she was completely healed. All pain was gone and she walked normally for the first time in many years. Praise God!

For years we have said to sick people that they could get healed – if only they had enough faith. **I tell you that it does not have to be the sick person that has the faith.** It just has to be someone in the equation that has it. I know there are several scriptures that have been used to propagate the wrong teaching – the teaching that the sick person has to be the one with the faith. We will look at them one by one in a later section.

Also in this passage in James, we find kind of an odd instruction. *"Confess your faults one to another, and pray one for another, that ye may be healed."* How can confessing our faults bring healing? *to cure*

This word faults is the Greek word *paraptoma*. It means a side slip (lapse or deviation), (unintentional) error or (willful) transgression. We are talking about spiritual error or what we call sin. Still, how can confessing our sins to one another get us healed?

There is a whole section in this book that deals with this very issue. All believers were to lay hands on the sick and see them recover. Since sin can be the root of an illness, by letting someone help us deal with the sin, they can help us recover. Remove the sin and the body can usually heal itself.

---

41 James 5:14-16

42 Exodus 30:23-25

43 Exodus 30:32

Breath of God

Your words have power.

In just a couple of chapters, I am going to make the amazing (almost unbelievable) statement that you have the power to command someone's body to change. You will never believe me unless you get this next truth. This truth will change your life if you will grab hold of it.

You are not alive because you have a heart and lungs and a brain. You are alive because you have the breath of God. God reached down, scooped up some dirt, and formed Adam. At that moment Adam had everything. He had a heart, he had lungs; he had everything. Even though he was a complete human being, he wasn't alive until God leaned down and breathed into Adam's nostrils – and then man became a living soul.[44] The reason you are alive today is not because your heart works. The reason you are alive today is because you have the breath of God.

It will be no surprise to most believers that the Hebrew word *ruwach* is translated into English as both Spirit and breath. You can see a clear example of this in Job 27:3-4, *"All the while my breath is in me..."* and Job 26:4 *"...and whose spirit came from you."* Both these words breath and spirit in these verses are the same word; *neshamah*. The Hebrew word *ruwach* is also translated as both spirit and breath. Compare Exodus 31:3, *"And I have filled him with the spirit of God..."* with Job 12:10, *"In whose hand is the soul of every living thing, and the breath of all mankind."* **The power of God, the Spirit of God, is in your breath!**

Job had this revelation when he said, *"The Spirit of God has made me and the breath of God gives me life."*[45] That is why God told us that the power of life and death is in our tongue.[46] You have the power of life and death because you speak with the breath of God. **We bless and we curse with the breath of God.** We bless or curse our children with the breath of God. *That's why of words are creative.*

Just because you don't see the effect today does not mean it is not there. When Jesus cursed the fig tree it still looked the same for a short period of time. But soon afterward, as the disciples passed the tree, they noted that it was dying.

The scriptures also tell us that we will be judged by our words.[47] I believe it is because we speak those words with the breath of God. We must give an account for every idle word we speak.[48]

King David declared, *"Let everything that has breath praise the Lord."*[49] Why does God desire our praise? When we praise Him, we are retuning His breath to Him. That breath of God cuts through the heavenlies, makes a path, and returns to God Himself. Who will stop God's breath from returning to Him? I dare say, no one. This is the reason why idolatry is such an abomination to God. You are praising something with the breath of God and giving it power.

I believe David had a real revelation about this. He also said, *"... and when my days are at an end you take my breath away."*[50] That's how a Christian should die. We should not die from sickness and disease. When our days are at an end, God takes back His breath.

Here are some scriptures that confirm the power you have because of God's breath in you.

God's breath gives life.
- Genesis 2:7 – God breathed on Adam and he became a living soul.
- Job 33:4 – The spirit of God has made me and the breath of God gives me life.
- Isaiah 42:5 – God has given breath to the people

You have ultimate power when you speak.
- Proverbs 18:21 – Life and death are in the power of tongue

We bless and curse with the breath of God.
- Mark 11:20-21 – When Jesus cursed something, it died
- The fig tree withered at the roots by His word

You are accountable for your words.
- Matt 12:36 – You will give an account for every idle word spoken
- Matt 12:37 – We will be judged by your words

Praise returns God's breath to him.
- Psalms 150:6 – let everything that has breath praise the Lord.
- Idol worship is so offensive to God for this reason.

When our days are at an end, He takes our breath away.
- Psalms 104:29 – when my life is at an end you take my breath away.
- Job 9:18 – He will not suffer me to take my breath away.
- Job 12:10 – In whose hand is the soul ... and the

breath of all mankind.
- Job 15:30 – by the breath of his mouth shall he go away.

This is why your words have power. You speak them with the breath/Spirit of God. That's why you'll have whatsoever you say. **Whatever you speak will come to pass in your life someday.** If you don't like what you have, check what you have been saying. You will have whatsoever you say.[51]

---

[44] Genesis 2:7

[45] Job 33:4

[46] Proverbs 18:21

[47] Matthew 12:37

[48] Matthew 12:36

[49] Psalms 150:6

[50] Psalms 104:29

[51] Mark 11:23

Section 3

Fixing the Error

Problem Scriptures – Old Testament

God is not the author of sickness & disease.

God wants everyone to be healed.

I am sure those statements bring to mind several contro-versial Bible passages that seem to point to the contrary. In this chapter we will examine many of the common scriptures people use to try to disprove the statements above.

What about Job?

One of the most common verses people use to try to prove that God does not always heal is found in Job. Let's look at the story in detail. Job was a godly man and there-fore enjoyed the protection and prosperity of God. Satan had no way to get to Job because of the wall of protection God had placed around him.

When God gave His permission for Job to be tested, Satan still had to find a legal way to attack Job. Satan cannot just jump on you for no reason. Satan did find a legal way to attack Job, as we read in Job 3:25:

"For the thing which I greatly feared is come upon me, and that which I was afraid of is come unto me."

Job had a fear. Not just a small fear, but a great fear. The very thing he feared is the "door" that Satan used. In later chapters I discuss the door to sickness and disease which is held open by wrong emotions. These wrong emotions can lead to demonic bondage. Specifically, skin diseases are often associated with fear. In Job's case, Satan could have chosen any illness to put on Job, but he had to have an entrance and he found it in fear, so he used a skin disease to afflict him.

I found a connection between fear and skin diseases several years ago when I was praying for someone. It came by a word of knowledge. Since that time, I have found several confirmations that these two things are connected. I cannot explain the physiological reasons for it, but medical science confirms it. Dermatologist will now tell you that certain skin conditions will get worse when you are under stress. Stress comes from fearing a particular outcome. Rev. Henry Wright mentions the same connection in his book, <u>A More Excellent Way</u>.[52]

At first glance it does seem that God was a bit slow to heal Job. Why the delay? Remember I said earlier that there may be a spiritual root to the illness, and/or there may be a spiritual blockage to the healing. For Job, both were true. The fear was the root of the illness. Then once he was in trouble, he created a blockage by what he said.

The story starts out with three of Job's friends trying to "comfort" him by telling him that he must have sinned for such calamity to come to him. They threw out all sorts of likely causes... all of them wrong. Suddenly a young man named Elihu spoke up. He must have been listening all along. Elihu scolded the three friends, *"because they found no answer, and yet had condemned Job."*[53]

But first, Elihu unloaded on Job. *"Against Job was his wrath kindled, because he (Job) justified himself rather than God."*[54] Elihu further accused Job and said, *"For he (Job) has said, It profits a man nothing that he should delight himself with God."*[55]

When God finally spoke, He reproved Job and the three friends, but not Elihu. It appears that what Elihu said was true.

Job had both a spiritual root to his illness and a spiritual blockage to his healing. God promised healing to Job if he would pray for his friends. Job got himself a bit of faith, acted on that *rhema* and was healed.

How do I know he had faith? Faith is revealed by actions. Faith without works is dead (non-existent).[56] You can only know that there is faith, if there is action. Because Job did pray for his friends according to the *rhema*, his actions revealed his faith.

Sickness is punishment

Another scripture that seems to be in conflict with our opening statements is found in Exodus. A surface analysis might seem to indicate that God punished people with sickness and disease. Consider Exodus 15:26

> *"And said, If you wilt diligently hearken to the voice of the LORD thy God, and wilt do that which is right in his sight, and will give ear to his commandments, and keep all his statutes, I will put none of these diseases upon thee, which I have brought upon the Egyptians: for I am the LORD that heals you."*

It sure looks like God is the author of sickness, since He

told them He would not put any on them. This is, however, a superficial understanding of the Word.

First of all, this is the Old Testament. Almost everyone who understands the Bible and the work of Jesus will admit that our covenant changed from the Old Testament to the New Testament. In fact, the word "Testament" means "Covenant" – Old Covenant and New Covenant. You cannot look at the way God dealt with people in the Old Covenant and say that is what we should expect today. Earlier in this book I explained Isaiah 53 in great detail. Jesus died that you might live, and He was wounded that you might be healed. People did not have this promise in the Old Testament, but we do in our New Covenant.

Let's look again at this verse in Exodus. I absolutely do not want to leave you with the impression that God's grand plan was to use sickness and disease as a form of punishment. This passage is known theologically as the ninth covenant of God towards man.[57] By studying covenants you will learn that covenants were not unique to the Hebrews. They existed in all cultures of the time. People would make covenant with each other and with their gods.

There were elements that were common to all covenants, and without them, it was not a valid covenant. Two such elements were blessings and curses. The party offering the covenant would tell the other party what they could expect in the way of blessings if they honored the covenant. There was also a clause that detailed what curses they could expect if they broke the covenant. One such example is found in Deuteronomy 28. It starts out by saying,

"And it shall come to pass if you shall listen diligently unto the voice of the Lord your God and observe and to do all his commandments, which I command you this day, that the Lord your God will set you on high above all nations of the earth: And all these blessings

shall come on you, and overtake you,..."

Then you see the counterpart to this covenant blessing – the covenant curses. Verse 45 of the same chapter says,

"Moreover all these curses shall come upon you, and shall pursue you, and overtake you, till you be destroyed, because you have not listened to the Lord your God to keep his commandments and his statutes which he commanded you."

This is standard contractual language for covenants. The covenant was not considered valid without such language. In most covenants, in most cultures, sickness, disease, and death were the most common curses of a covenant.

It is also important to note that **it was not the covenant writer that would bring the sickness and disease.** It was simply an invitation for sickness and disease to come if the covenant was broken. These same curses were common in covenants among all men. How could a man cause sickness to come on another man? It is plain to see that it would be some non-human entity that would fulfill the curse when we are talking about men. Typically the god that the parties served would be the one expected to fulfill the blessings or curses.

We should think the same of God's covenants as well. The sickness was NOT a result of God deciding one day that He was fed up with Israel's behavior and determining to punish them. **The invitation was issued, in the spirit realm, for sickness and disease to come because of the actions of the covenant breaker.** God was the overseer of the covenant and therefore it was His obligation to see that the terms of the contract or covenant were carried out.

In the verse I mentioned earlier from Exodus 15, God was reiterating the curse for breaking covenant, not putting forth some new doctrine of punishment. In this same verse in Exodus, God declares, "I am the God that heals you." So when the curse came, as a provision of the covenant, then God healed them.

Theologically speaking, this is exactly what happened to mankind. We broke the Old Covenant and the curses that were contained therein came into our lives. There was a penalty of sickness and death. But because God did not want us to suffer such things, He sent His own Son to pay the penalty of the curse for us all.

Now the curse is broken for those of us who could not live up to the Old Covenant, with its 612 laws. Our new covenant has a remedy for the curses: *"Christ has redeemed us from the curse of the law, being made a curse for us..."*[58]

The Apostle Paul said it so perfectly: *"For the wages of sin is death; but the gift of God is eternal life through Jesus Christ our Lord."*[59]

The word "wages" means "the ration or paycheck of a soldier." Sickness and disease is our compensation for the path we have chosen. But Jesus took that compensation (paycheck of sin) and gave us His paycheck for righteousness.

The curse of our previous covenant (Old Testament) included sickness, disease, and death. It was the portion of all who broke the law. God was bound by covenant to the blessings or curses contained within the covenant.

Now, however, we have a better system. The curse for breaking covenant was laid on Jesus. That included all our sickness and diseases. For these reasons, we cannot look at Old Testament scripture to form our doctrine of healing under the New Testament dispensation.

---

[52] Wright, Henry, A More Excellent Way, Pleasant Valley Publications, Thomaston, GA, 2002, 234-235.

[53] Job 32:3

[54] Job 32:2

[55] Job 34:9

[56] James 2:17

[57] Dake, Finish Hennings, Dake's Annotated Reference Bible", Dake Bible Sales Inc., Lawrenceville, GA, 1963, 57

[58] Galatians 3:13

[59] Romans 6:23

Problem Scriptures – New Testament

Most of the objections I have heard about God's ability or desire to heal us today are born out of people's experiences, not out of theology. Someone will tell me that their mother was a godly woman and she died of cancer. Someone else will tell me how they have had faith for healing for years and yet they have grown sicker and sicker. I find that most people who do not believe in healing today have formed their doctrine out of their own disappointments, rather than from the Word of God.

Then there are people who believe God heals some people some times. Again, they are influenced by their own experiences, or the experiences of others.

If you only have enough faith...

Misinterpretation of Scripture has been a big contributor to the development of wrong doctrines about healing. We were taught for many years that, if you just had enough faith, you could be healed. This teaching came out of the great faith movement of the 60's and 70's, and I thank God for that movement. However, this doctrine was missing a couple of key elements, elements which I will point out in later paragraphs. Proponents of this doctrine used some of the following scriptures to make their point.

Matthew 9:22 – The woman with the issue of blood was healed. Jesus told her that her faith had made her whole. By the way, this word "whole" is the Greek word *sozo,* which I defined earlier. Notice that Jesus did not have to command her healing or cast anything out of her. She used her own faith and so Jesus had to do NOTHING.

Luke 18:38 – The blind man received his sight. Jesus said, "Receive your sight; your faith has saved you." He did not command anything or cast out anything. He merely informed the man that his own faith had saved him. Please note that the word "saved" here is also *sozo.*

Matthew 15:28 – The Syrophenician woman's daughter had a demon. Jesus did not want to minister to her. Since this was a demonic issue, Jesus was most likely concerned about how the girl would stay free. Remember, when Jesus cast a demon out of a man, He said,

> *"When the unclean spirit is gone out of a man, he walks through dry places seeking rest and finds none. Then he says, 'I will return unto my house from where I came out' and, when he arrives, he finds it empty, swept, and garnished. Then he goes and takes with himself seven other spirits more wicked than himself and they enter in and dwell there and the last state of that man is worse than the first."[60]*

This woman was not a Jew. She did not have the law to guide her behavior. We assume Jesus did not want to do deliverance because it was unlikely the girl could stay free, and then she would be worse off.

Yet, notice what Jesus said to her: *"O woman, great is your faith; be it unto you even as you will."*

Again, Jesus did not lay hands on her daughter or cast out a demon. He did not minister to her. He simply declared that she could have whatever she wanted because she had her own faith.

Mark 5:36 –A 12 year old girl was dead. Jesus told the father to "only believe." This seems to have been more of a comforting statement than a requirement because the Bible does not say whether the father was able to conjure up any of his own faith or not. It is clear from Jesus' statement that the father did not have his own at that time. It was sort of like saying, "Don't worry, she will be fine."

Next, Jesus put the mourners out of the room before he ministered to the girl. Now, I have also heard people say that Jesus had to put people out of the room because they did not have faith, but this is not what the Bible says. In verse 38, we find the reason why they were put out. It says they were weeping and wailing. This word "wailing" is *alalazo*, which means to utter (something) or cry out loudly and vehemently, especially in protest. There is power in our words. **They were speaking against what Jesus was trying to do.** It was not their lack of faith – it was the fact that they were using their words against the efforts of healing.

Luke 17:19 – The leper was healed. Jesus had just healed 10 lepers. One of them was a Samaritan. This man could not go to the temple as Jesus had instructed because he was not Jewish. As soon as he realized he was healed, he returned to glorify God. Jesus then said to him, "Your *faith has made you whole.*"

It should be no surprise to you by this time that the word "whole" is the word *sozo*. The man was already healed, and, yet, Jesus said that his faith had earned him the "whole package." This means that the man got something with his own faith that he did not get from Jesus. He not only received healing; he was made completely whole because of his own faith.

I want to make a point so that we don't get off into some new (wrong) doctrine. There were times when Jesus ministered to (laid hands on) people who had their own faith. **I am not saying that if you have your own faith, then no one should pray for you**. I mean to say that if you have your own faith, you CAN be healed without anyone else praying for you.

Consider the healing of the blind man. The story is told in Matthew 20:34 and in Mark 10:52. It may be the same story in Luke 18:42, but that is not clear. Matthew and Mark both say that Jesus was leaving Jericho when it happened. Luke seems to tell the same story, but he says that they were coming near to, or approaching, Jericho.

In Matthew the author records that Jesus laid hands on the blind eyes. Mark does not give that detail. Mark quotes Jesus as saying, "Go your way; your faith has made you whole." Obviously, the man had his own faith, yet Jesus touched his eyes anyway.

The important point to take away from this section is this: **Jesus did not depend on other people's faith. He was the minister and He expected to be the one with the faith.** When others had their own faith, He did not have to use His faith. When someone did have their own faith, He pointed it out – like it was part of the lesson: "Get your own faith and you can have whatever you want."

Matthew 8:5-13 In the story of the centurion's servant, the centurion had his own faith. Jesus was ready to go to his home to minister, but the centurion made it clear that was not necessary. *"Just speak a word,"* he said.

You can almost hear some surprise in Jesus' voice here. He said to the centurion. *"I say unto you, I have not found so great faith, no, not in Israel."*[61]

He was not used to people having or using their own faith. When someone had their own faith, Jesus was quick to point it out and remind them that they could have whatever they needed because they had their own faith.

Let's return to the passage to which I have referred several times already. Matthew 17:20 tells the story of the disciples who could not cast the demon out of the boy. **Jesus told them that since they were the ministers, they were expected to have faith for the one to whom they ministered.** Then He told them that if they had their own faith, *"Nothing will be impossible to you."*

There were several times when Jesus had to use His own faith as the minister. Here are some examples.

Luke 7:12-15 – Jesus raised a man from the dead. In this case it does not appear that anyone involved, except Jesus, had their own faith. Certainly, the dead man did not have faith.

John 9:1-7 – Jesus healed a man that was blind from birth. The man did not ask for healing. When asked about it later, he declared that he did not even know who healed him. He referred to Jesus a prophet. The man did not have any faith of his own.

John 11:1-44 – Jesus raised Lazarus from the dead. The dead man had no faith. The people standing around mourning had no faith. Even Lazarus' sisters had no faith, because they told Jesus that if he had come earlier, their brother would have recovered.

Is it God's Will?

Some people are not sure it is God's will that all are healed. I admit it would be hard to have faith if you were not sure where God stood on the issue. Some of the verses below have been interpreted in such a way that they have brought doubt and confusion. Let's take a fresh look at them.

Mark 1:40-42 – A leper came to Jesus and said, *"If you will, you can make me clean."* Jesus said, *"I will, be clean."* Some people use this scripture to develop a wrong doctrine or prayer. They argue that based on this scripture, we should ask God to heal us and we should pray, "Lord, if it be your will, please heal us."

The word "clean" in this passage is the Greek word *katharizo* and it means to cleanse. It does not mean to heal. It was never translated heal or healing in the New Testament. It was always translated cleanse, purify, purge etc. A good example of the way this word was used when talking about something other than leprosy is found in 1 John 1;9,

> *"If we confess our sins, he is faithful and just to forgive us our sins and to <u>cleanse</u> us from all unrighteousness."*

Leprosy was called the "Strike of God.' It was a sign of sin. The first person to get leprosy was Miriam, the sister of Moses.[62] She was stricken with it because of her sin of rebellion against Moses. The rabbis had been given many remedies and cures, but there was no biblical cure for leprosy, because it was the strike of God. They believed that only Messiah could cure leprosy because any cure would have to include remission of sin.

When the man approached Jesus, he did not ask to be healed, or cured, or any of the other words we associate with healing. He asked to be spiritually purified. Throughout the New Testament, this word is consistently used to speak of spiritual cleansing – not healing. When the man declared that Jesus could cleanse him if he wished, he was making a declaration that Jesus was the Messiah – that he had the power to forgive sins. In the same way that Jesus never refuses us spiritual cleansing, He never refuses us healing. The reason the man even asked, was that he was not intimately familiar with Jesus or God, and was not sure if He would do it. It was more of an indictment of his own knowledge of God – he did not know God well enough to know if he could be cleansed – than it was a question about Jesus' willingness. Since we have the luxury of the whole Bible, we have no excuse to wonder weather it is God's will to heal us. He has made his will perfectly known. He called himself Jehovah Rapha, "I am the Lord that heals you." Jesus healed EVERY SINGLE PERSON who asked him. He was wounded so that you could count on your healing.

One last thought about this verse. Notice that the leper and Jesus were both dealing with a spiritual issue – cleansing. Jesus agreed to spiritually purify or cleanse him. Once that sin was removed, the body was instantly healed. **Deal with the soul and the body can recover.**

Does God Heal Through Doctors?

1Timothy 5:23 *"Drink no longer water, but use a little wine for thy stomach's sake and your often infirmities."* Some people have used this verse as a foundation for their claims that God does not always want to heal everyone.

They say that God would rather have us use medicine or other natural remedies to control illness.

I believe that the verse proves the opposite. This verse is not proof that God does not want to heal, but rather that God wants everyone healed and that his methods may vary, but the desire is consistent. If God did not want Timothy healed, why bother to tell him to drink wine. There are a variety of potential infirmities that might be remedied by the alcohol in the wine. God wants us all healed so much that he uses a variety of means to ensure that all have the opportunity. Not everyone is a believer and they do not go to church. How then can they call for the elders to anoint them with oil?

When people use this verse to make the claim that God did not want to heal Timothy, I would ask them if they have ever taken an herbal remedy for an illness. How about chicken soup for a cold? Would that mean that you are working against the will of God? If you do not believe that God wants to heal you every time, then why take any medicine or go to a doctor? Why not sit home and see if this is the time that God will heal you? If God does not want to heal you every time, and you go to a doctor and get healed, then might you have worked against the divine will of God?

People who think that God does not want to heal may have limited the concept of healing to a miracle. They will only give God the credit if they witness a miracle. Actually, this does not agree with the Scriptures. Mark 16:18 tells us to lay hands on the sick and they will recover. Recovery is a process, not an event. Most of the people who get healed in this ministry recover over a matter of days rather than a matter of minutes. Of course, we often see the dramatic miracles, but we can never count on it. When I pray for people, I tell them, "You will be healed. I never know whether it will be a miracle, or a recovery, but it will happen, one way or the other."

God Uses Natural Remedies

I was asked to pray for a Doctor who needed healing. That was a bit intimidating. He had an anxiety disorder and he was taking medication for it. Also, he could not sleep at night. Understand that I have no medical training. I began praying for him and I heard the Lord say to command his serotonin levels. Since I had no idea what serotonin was, I did not know whether to command it to go up or down. I asked the doctor if it was ok to do this and he agreed. I commanded his serotonin to be manufactured in the proper amount and for it to stay at the proper levels. Then, as I was just about to finish, I heard the Lord say, "Tell him to eat apples." Frankly, I felt foolish but, I have learned to know what the voice of the Lord sounds like on the inside of me. I told him that the Lord wanted him to eat apples.

After we finished our prayers, the doctor told me that the medicine he was taking was designed to inhibit the uptake of serotonin and make it available longer in his system. Bull's eye! He did not know what the apple had to do with his problem. I got on the internet and searched it out. We found that apples, when eaten before bedtime, promote restful sleep. He bought apples and ate them. He told me that he had the most restful sleep he had experienced in a long time. Praise God!

Do you think that maybe some of the things we find on our planet are here by accident? Perhaps God designed a whole ecosystem that is meant to support our lives. I believe in natural cures. I believe that God uses the things found in nature to heal and restore us. This is the way I like to think of it. God wanted us all healed so much. He knew that we would not all go to church and have an understanding of divine healing so he furnished the earth with things that could bring healing. He also wanted us all healed so much that he gave wisdom to doctors. Do you really think that the knowledge in medical technology came from the wisdom of man? I do not believe we are capable of such wisdom, apart from God. If you look at the nations that have excluded the God of Abraham, Isaac, and Jacob, you do not find scientific breakthroughs and new patents being registered. These are found in the predominately Christian nations.

There is one other issue I want to address in this chapter. It is not so much a scriptural interpretation. As a mater of fact, as far as I am aware, the next argument against divine healing is not supported by any scripture, other than perhaps Paul's thorn. I have devoted a whole chapter in this book to that misinterpretation.

God Does Not Send Sickness For the Purpose of Teaching Us

I have heard many people say that God sends sickness and disease to people to teach them a lesson. Then they usually tell their own tale of how they had a sickness and God spoke to them through that disease and they learned a valuable lesson. This is not only wrong, but I would imagine the very thought of it would be an affront to God. Let me ask you a series of questions. Does sickness and disease exist in heaven? No. Did it exist in the Garden of Eden? No. It is clear that sickness and disease entered the world with sin. Sickness is the by-product of sin. I will say it over and over in this book. You can easily determine what is a work of Satan, and what is a work of God.

> "...For this purpose the Son of God was manifested, that he might destroy the works of the devil." [63]

It is childishly easy. Take a look at what Jesus destroyed, and you will be able to determine what is "a work of the devil." Jesus destroyed sin, sickness, disease, demonic power, and false teaching. All of these are therefore the work of the devil, not the work of God.

Law of First Mention

On that note, let's look at the connection between sin and sickness. Theologians agree that the book of Job is the oldest book in the Bible. By this I mean that it was written before any other book. Obviously, the events did not occur first, but these were the first to be recorded. This is important because it influences our interpretation.

In theological study, there is a principle called the "Law of First Mention." This means when interpreting Scripture, the first time a thing is mentioned, everything about that situation should be considered significant. The way in which the thing is first presented is the way in which it should be interpreted unless there are some unusual circumstances.

In the book of Job, we find the first account of sickness ever written. If you study this account, it is easy to determine that the sickness Job experienced clearly came from Satan. Satan did not convince God to put sickness on Job, but rather, he convinced God to let him put it on Job. The sickness was a work of the enemy. It did not originate with God.

In the Old Testament, in its current order, the first time the word sickness or disease appears was in Genesis 48:1. Here Joseph is told that his father is sick. The word used here is the Hebrew word *chalah* and can also be translated as worn out. This is not a clear usage since it might simply mean that Jacob was ready to die of old age. The next occurrences are related to women having their menstrual cycle. While they had a flow of blood, they were called "sick." You can see an example of this in Leviticus 20:18.

The first time we hear of a "healing" in the Old Testament, God healed Abimelech, his wife, and his maidservants. Why did they need healing? They were under a curse. Abimelech had taken Sarah for wife and this brought a curse of barrenness on everyone. The word for healed in this verse is the Hebrew word *rapha*. You may recognize it was one of the names of God. It means to mend or cure. I mention this because I want to make note of this fact. God treats healing from a curse or demonic affliction the same as healing from sickness.

Miriam needed healing from leprosy. In the story found in Numbers 12, the leprosy came about as a result of sin. Miriam spoke against her leader/brother. This sin brought a curse

The first time we see the use of the words sickness or disease, in the context of what we now consider to be illnesses, is in the book of Deuteronomy. There are several verses that refer to sickness. Remember that these verses in Deuteronomy are about God making covenant with Israel. In the context of covenant, God speaks blessings and curses. He tells Israel what they can expect in the way of blessings if they are obedient, and what will come upon them in the form of curses if they are disobedient. Remember, sickness and death were almost always a part of any covenant.

I don't want to get into a whole dissertation on covenants, but here is some critical information. This type of covenant we find in Deuteronomy was called a suzerainty covenant. This means that there is one party with plenary power. The party with the power writes the covenant and the other party only has the right to say yes or no, but cannot change the terms or conditions of the covenant. The parties would then call upon God to enforce the provisions of the covenant; to watch over it and see that justice is served according to the terms of the covenant. IN THIS ROLE ONLY, does the Lord talk about putting diseases or not putting diseases on His people. When Israel broke covenant with God in the Old Testament, the curse of sickness came upon them. According to the provisions of the covenant, God was obligated to enforce the blessings and curses based on the people's performance. At no other place, and under no other condition other than covenant, does God talk about having a role in the sickness and disease of His people other than to heal them.

In the New Testament (New Covenant) we are not help-less victims of the effects of curses, which might include sickness. Galatians 3:13 says that Jesus redeemed us from the curse of the law, being made a curse for us.

Back to the argument.... God does not put sickness and disease on us to teach us a lesson. There are God ordained ways for believers to be trained. First and foremost, the Bible tells us that:

The Holy Spirit Is The Teacher.

➤ **Luke 12:12** *"For the Holy Ghost shall teach you in the same hour what ye ought to say."*

➤ **John 14:26** *"But the Comforter, which is the Holy Ghost, whom the Father will send in my name, he shall teach you all things, and bring all things to your remem-brance, whatsoever I have said unto you."*

➤ **1 Corinthians 2:13** *"Which things also we speak, not in the words which man's wisdom teaches, but which the Holy Ghost teaches; comparing spiritual things with spiritual."*

The Word of God Should Teach Us.

➤ **2 Timothy 3:16** *"All scripture is given by inspiration of God, and is profitable for doctrine, for reproof, for correction, for instruction in righteousness:"*

Spiritual Leaders And Pastors Should Teach Us.

➤ **1 Corinthians 12:28** *"And God hath set some in the church, first apostles, secondarily prophets, thirdly* teachers, after that miracles, then gifts of healings, helps, governments, diversities of tongues."

➤ **Ephesians 4:11** *"And he gave some, apostles; and some, prophets; and some, evangelists; and some, pastors and teachers; for the equipping of the saints."*

➤ **Colossians 1:28** *"Whom we preach, warning every man, and teaching every man in all wisdom; that we may present every man perfect in Christ Jesus:"*

➤ **Colossians 3:16** *"Let the word of Christ dwell in you richly in all wisdom; teaching and admonishing one another in psalms and hymns and spiritual songs, singing with grace in your hearts to the Lord."*

If people tell me that the Lord had to give them cancer in order for them to learn to trust Him, or God put them flat on their backs in bed to teach them something, it says to me that they do not know the voice of the Holy Spirit, or they do not listen. They do not know the Word, or search out answers from the Word, in their time of need. They do not receive teaching by other believers or leaders. All of these are the God-ordained ways to be instructed by the Lord.

There is no scripture in the Bible that says God puts sickness and disease on His people to teach them a lesson. Not only is that a false teaching, but it distorts the nature and character of God. God calls Himself Jehovah Rapha. Jesus suffered a tortuous death that you might be healed. It is not scripturally sound to say that it is God's will for anyone to be sick.

Don't we wish that God got everything that was His will? He said that He wanted all to be saved.

"This is good, and it pleases God our Savior, who wants everyone to be saved and to come to the knowledge of the truth."[64] (American Standard Bible)

It is plain that it is God's will for all to be saved, yet we know that there are people who die without being saved. If someone does not get saved, it is not God's fault. We each have our own choice. It is also the will of God for all to be healed, yet all are not.

Our free will applies just as much to our health as it does to our salvation. God has given us instructions on how to live in health. Proverbs 14:30 says, *"A sound heart is the life of the flesh: but envy the rottenness of the bones."* Yet, in spite of this warning, people will allow envy in their soul and their bones begin to decay. Then they say that it is either God's fault that they are sick or God's will that they are not healed. Go figure....

---

[60] Matthew 12:43-45

[61] Luke 7:9

[62] Numbers 12:10

[63] 1 John 3:8

[64] 2 Timothy 2:3-4

Paul's Thorn

"And lest I should be exalted above measure through the abundance of the revelations, there was given to me a thorn in the flesh, the messenger of Satan to buffet me, lest I should be exalted above measure."[65]

Was Paul's thorn in the flesh sickness or disease? Did Paul really suffer from an incurable eye disease? Is it true that God refused to heal Paul of this eye disease, even though Paul prayed repeatedly? The answer to these questions is a firm NO!

Follow with me...

The first law of proper Biblical exegesis (Critical explanation or analysis, especially of a text) is that you must determine what the word or phrase meant to the original audience. In the context of their culture and their literature, what would it have meant to them? We can find clues by looking at other documents of that era, or other documents that might have influenced the people of that era.

The first step in this kind of analysis is to look within the document itself to see if, perhaps, other occurrences of the same word or phrase might give us clues. In this case, Paul only used this phrase once in this letter.

The next step then is to see how the writer might have used this word or phrase in other writings. Again, in this case, Paul never used the phrase "thorn in the flesh" in any of his other writings. He did however use the word "buffet."

1 Cor 4:11

"Even unto this present hour we both hunger, and thirst, and are naked, and are buffeted, and have no certain dwelling place; And labor, working with our own hands: being reviled, we bless; being persecuted, we suffer it: Being defamed, we intreat: we are made as the filth of the world, and are the off scouring of all things unto this day."[66]

Paul not only used the word, but expanded his description to include a definition. He listed the ways in which they were buffeted, and the list does not include sickness or disease.

Next, we look at what historical or cultural influences were present in Paul's life that might have caused him to use this word or phrase. BINGO!

Paul was a scholar. In fact, he was trained as a Pharisee by one of the most brilliant scholars of his time, Gamaliel. Paul would have been greatly influenced in his speech and writings by his studies of the Old Testament.

This leads me nicely to the next level of interpretation, which is within the Bible as a whole. This is a textbook-perfect example of how two methods of Biblical exegesis collide. The proper way to find out what the phrase meant is to look internally, meaning within the Bible. (We only really want go outside the Bible if the word or phrase appears nowhere else, or is vague.) Usually, we are able to identify how the author intended to use it:

➤ based on other of his works, or
➤ by identifying the factors that influenced him, or
➤ we find it in other places in the Bible.

We know what might have influenced Paul at the time, but then we have to make sure that using this interpretation would make the verse consistent with the rest of Scripture. The internal consistency of the Bible is one the foundations of the Christian (and Jewish) faith. We believe in the inerrancy of the Word. If there appears to be a conflict, then we failed in our analysis somewhere.

Paul was both influenced by the Old Testament, and his words can also be found in the Old Testament. His audience would also have been familiar with the Old Testament. That makes this so easy. That means we have every reason to believe that Paul would have used the term in a manner consistent with Old Testament writings.

So, we look to the Old Testament to see how others used this word "thorn." Remember we are looking for the figurative use of the word, not the literal. (As far as I know there is no one who believes that Paul had a literal thorn in his flesh.) By the way, those who try to interpret the thorn as sickness are agreeing that the thorn is figurative.

Here are some of the Old Testament figurative references to thorns:

• **Numbers 33:55** *But if ye will not drive out the inhabitants of the land from before you; then it shall come to pass, that those which ye let remain of them shall be pricks in your eyes, and thorns in your sides, and shall vex you in the land wherein ye dwell.*

• **Joshua 23:13** *Know for a certainty that the Lord your*

God will no more drive out any of these nations from before you; but they shall be snares and traps unto you, and scourges in your sides, and <u>thorns in your eyes</u>, until ye perish from off this good land which the Lord your God hath given you.

- **Judges 2:3** *Wherefore I also said, I will not drive them out from before you; but they shall be as <u>thorns in your sides</u>, and their gods shall be a snare unto you.*

- **2 Samuel 23:6** *But the sons of Belial shall be all of them as <u>thorns</u> thrust away, because they cannot be taken with hands:*

Proper Biblical exegesis dictates that **a word or phrase cannot mean to us what it could never have meant to the original hearers.**

For example, Psalms 139:13 says, *"For you O Lord have possessed my reins..."* The unscholarly reader might look at this and think that this is the same word as the reins of a horse. This would mean that God possesses my reins, or my restraint. But NO!

This word "reins" is an old English word, which means "inward parts." This word in Hebrew is *kilyah*. It has nothing whatsoever to do with the reins of a horse or any kind of restraint. Since this word *kilyah* could never have meant "restraint" to the original audience, it cannot now legitimately be interpreted to mean "restraint" to us.

So it is with Paul's thorn. Never, in the entire Bible, was the word "thorn" used for "sickness" or "disease," literally or figuratively. Therefore, it could not have meant that to the hearers of Paul's words either. Figuratively, this word was used to describe people, or groups of people, who were aggravating or harassing. This interpretation certainly seems to fit the life of Paul as we know it....beaten, thrown in jail, stoned and left for dead. Yes, this certainly fits.

Not only does it fit the life of Paul; it fits the context of his words and it fits with all the proper elements of scholarly Biblical interpretation.

- Paul said that his thorn was a messenger of Satan (angel of the Devil). This word "messenger" is the Greek word *angelos*. It appears 188 times in the Bible, and is translated "angel" 181 times and "messenger" the other 7 times. In all the 188 times in the entire Bible, it is always used to describe a being, not a thing.[67]

- Paul not only tells us that it was a being, but describes the mission of the being; to buffet him. This word "buffet" means "to strike blow after blow." Rotherham translates it, *"that he might be buffeting me."*[68] The word buffet means repeated battering, as when the waves buffet a boat, or as when they buffeted Jesus:[69]

  > *"And some began to spit on him, and to cover his face, and to buffet him, and to say unto him, Prophesy: and the servants did strike him with the palms of their hands."* [70]

  Notice how Rotherham uses the personal pronoun "he" when translating this passage. Likewise, Weymouth translates this as, *"Satan's angel dealing blow after blow."* (Weymouth New Testament) Both of these translators chose the personal pronoun "he" when translating this verse. Buffeting was never a word used in connection with sickness – it was a word used in connection with people who repeated attacked or aggravated.

- Paul's use of the words "thorn" and "buffet" is both consistent with other New Testament writers (see again Mark

14:65), and with Old Testament writers (see above list).

Now we come to another argument that is often used in defense of the wrong interpretation regarding Paul's sickness:

Gal 4:13-15

> *"You know how through infirmity of the flesh I preached the gospel unto you at the first. And my temptation which was in my flesh you despised not, nor rejected; but received me as an angel of God, even as Christ Jesus. Where is then the blessedness you spoke of? for I bear you record, that, if it had been possible, you would have plucked out your own eyes, and have given them to me."*[71]

At first glace, it might sound like Paul had a sickness in his eyes. But we can only get to that conclusion based on our bias.

To prove that we can have interpretive bias, let me propose the following hypothetical interpretation, which I am not even remotely suggesting is true: On the road to Damascus, Paul was blinded by the Lord, right? He was blinded because he had a personal encounter with the Lord, and he stayed blind until the prophet came and prayed for him.

Other than Adam in the Garden of Eden, only one other man in Scripture had a personal encounter with the Lord and actually saw Him. That man was Moses. After his encounter with the Lord, Moses, because his face shone, had to wear a veil over his face when talking to the people of Israel.

Suppose that the same thing happened to Paul's eyes; I might think they shone. Now, if I had interpretive bias, I might think that Paul and others thought that his shining eyes were an affliction. This interpretation might seem to fit the words, but it would only be interpretive bias.

Now let me offer you a more realistic and scholarly theory. Paul spoke of his "infirmity" in verse 13. The Greek word for "infirmity" here is *astheneia,* which means "feebleness (of body or mind)." He also said they did not despise or reject him because of the "temptation which was in my flesh." The Greek word for "temptation" in this verse is *peirasmos,* which Strong's Concordance tells us means "a putting to proof (by experiment [of good], experience [of evil], solicitation, discipline or provocation); by implication adversity." In other words, being proved by going through a hard time.

Scholars believe that Paul was probably preaching to the Galatians just after his stoning at Antioch. (You can find the story in Acts 14:19). They stoned him and left him for dead. Now, if Paul's next preaching assignment after this was to the Galatians, no wonder he called himself "feeble at the first." It would also explain his use of the word "temptation" or "proofing." God certainly "proofed" or "proved" Paul at Antioch. His faith and his work were put to the test. This possible explanation of this feebleness also fits Paul's other statement about the "thorn in the flesh," the messenger from Satan that buffeted him.

The sole verse on which most misinterpretations are based is the last one in this passage. *"For I bear you record, that, if it had been possible, you would have plucked out your own eyes, and have given them to me."*

Consider the possibility Paul was using this phrase in the same manner as we would say, "I know you would give me your right arm if you thought I needed it." In other words, could this have been a colloquialism?

Finally, even if we grant (and I don't) that Paul was sick in the sense of disease or illness, it is clear that is was for a time, and then he recovered. Let's assume for argument's sake that Paul had a sickness. Perhaps this is why he said in Galatians 4:13, *"You know how through infirmity of the flesh I preached the Gospel unto you at the first."*

Notice the last phrase, "at the first." He does not mean he preached the gospel "at the first," but that his infirmity was "at the first." And IF his infirmity was "at the first," it must not have lasted. Again, the reason I said, "IF we grant that Paul was sick," is because it is still not clear from this passage that he was sick at all. He was probably wounded and cut up and bruised from the stoning, but not sick.

Remember that I have presented the above statements for the purpose of presenting all interpretive possibilities of the passage. Reread the paragraph where I said I have a more realistic and scholarly interpretation. Then, if you still can't shake what you have been taught by tradition, I still say to you that if Paul had a sickness, he implied by his own choice of words that it was "at the first," and that he recovered. It was not related to the buffeting, which God refused to remove. That was a different issue.

The final test of one's interpretation is this: does this interpretation bring theological harmony or disharmony? Generally speaking, **if the interpretation brings theological disharmony, it should not be considered a valid interpretation.** Although there is not time in this book, I could go on for pages and pages about the theological harmony of the Old and New Testament proofs of God's desire to heal. In fact, I have given, at times, more than six hours of lectures on the subject.

The suggestion that Paul had an eye disease which God refused to heal brings such theological **disharmony** that one would have to change the interpretation of countless verses to approach anything resembling theological harmony.

I will give you just one example of how the wrong interpretation would bring theological disharmony. In Exodus 15:26 God declares Himself Jehovah *Rapha*... *"I am the Lord that heals you."* Since this is one of the names of God, it means that God doesn't just DO healing; He IS healing.

If God, Who is healing, refused to heal Paul, then we

would have to change our entire understanding of the nature and attributes of God. We could no longer say that He IS what His name implies, but rather... only sometimes He might DO what His name implies. Talk about major theological disharmony!

I say that the only way a person can justify the interpretation of Paul's "thorn" as "sickness" and his "infirmity" as an "eye disease" is if he or she is biased or predisposed to believe it. We cannot justify such an interpretation, either from the scriptures themselves or by applying sound Biblical exegesis.

---

[65] 2 Corinthians 12:7

[66] 1 Corinthians 4:11

[67] Bosworth, F.F., "Christ The Healer, Fleming H. Revell, a division of Baker Book House Co, Grand Rapids, MI 1973, 194

[68] Rotherham, Joseph Bryant,Rotherham Emphasized Bible, Grand Rapids, Michigan, Kregel Publications,1959,189

[69] Bosworth, 194

[70] Mark 14:65

[71] Galatians 4:13-15

Section 4

Enemy Intelligence Briefing

The Agreement That Costs You Your Health

I wish that walking in health was as easy as believing all the pages in this book up to this point. But there is more.

I am reminded of the scripture from Isaiah 53 that talks about those that are bruised. *"He was bruised for our iniquities."* That word bruised means "to break down", or in the personal sense, "I break down." Many of you have broken down, and not just on the outside, but on in the inside as well.

As I studied healing, searching for the hidden formula, I noticed an obvious, but often overlooked, reality. Much of the time when Jesus "healed" someone, He was really casting out a demon. An example of this is the woman with the spirit of infirmity that was bent over for 18 years.[72] Jesus had to cast out a demon to get her healed.

There were also many other instances of Jesus healing people by casting out a demon. Following are a couple of them that come to mind.

Luke 6:18 *"And they that were vexed with unclean spirits: and they were healed."*

Luke 9:42 *"And as he was yet a coming, the devil threw him down, and tare him. And Jesus rebuked the unclean spirit, and healed the child, and delivered him again to his father."*

This word "healed" is the Greek word *iaomai*. It means "to cure." The Bible uses this word to mean both physical healing and deliverance from a demon. You can find this same Greek word in Mark's story of the woman with the issue of blood:

Mark 5:29 *"And straightway the fountain of her blood was dried up; and she felt in her body that she was healed of that plague."*

This word "healed" is the same Greek word, *iaomai*. Jesus and his disciples made no distinction between curing an illness and casting out a demon. They called it all the same thing – healing.

I agree with the great Bible teacher Derek Prince's theological position on this issue. He said, "It is unscriptural to pray for the sick if one is not prepared also to cast out demons."[73] As we move on into the area of how to heal, you will find this bit of information invaluable.

Let's take a look at the connection between the demonic and sickness and disease. There was a woman bowed over with a spirit of infirmity for 18 years that Jesus healed by loosing her from the demon.[74] Jesus healed a paralyzed man by saying, "Your sins be forgiven you."[75] Jesus cast out a dumb spirit and a man could speak.[76]

In fact, sin was so much connected with sickness in Bible times that when the disciples came upon a man that was blind from birth, they asked Jesus, "Who sinned, this man or his parents?"[77] It was a well established belief of Biblical times that the soul was connected to the body.

The soul is where sin resides. It is where the enemy sets up his workshop. Once established in your soul, he begins to use your soul (your mind, will, and emotions) to produce harmful effects in your body.

Doctors have long known this link existed, but most of them have not made the spiritual connection. We all know, thanks to medical science, if you allow stress in your soul, you become a candidate for a heart attack. If you allow worry in your soul, you may expect ulcers.

Recently doctors have discovered that if you harbor anger, bitterness and resentment in your soul, you will get arthritis. The anger causes an over-production of a chemical. When you body cannot process the chemical fast enough, the excess is stored in your joints and causes your joints to be eaten away. As the Body of Christ, we are supposed to be, "... *fitly joined together, each joint supplying what is needed.*"[78] When we get "out of joint" with each other, our joints let us know it.

I can tell you story after story about people who were healed when they dealt with the issues of their soul. I was in Mexico teaching a school of healing. A woman came to be healed. She had such intense joint pain in her hips that she was having trouble walking. She walked very slowly; really she wobbled along.

We tried to kick out the pain, but it would not go. This is always a sign that the pain in the body is connected to a pain in the soul. I prayed and got a word of knowledge.

I told her that her soul was in pain because there was a family member on whom she felt she should have been able to depend, but that person had let her down. She was angry and would not forgive him. She admitted this was correct. I told her that the pain in her hips would not leave until she dealt with the issue of her soul. She refused.

As we were getting ready to close the meeting, she changed her mind. I guess the pain was so bad that she was willing to do anything. I told her to return the next day since it was late. The next day she came in jumping and skipping. She had repented by herself and cast out that spirit herself! As soon as she did, the pain left and all function returned to her joints.

Since we must be willing to deal with the issues of the soul in order to "Heal Them All," this book includes instruction in this area. We let a lot of spiritual junk in our souls that the enemy uses against us. We make an agreement with negative thoughts. The enemy uses these agreements to take over the rulership of a part of our souls.

The enemy is not the owner of our souls, but he is an occupying force. I use this word occupation from the military vocabulary, because I think it gives us the best picture of what is happening. The enemy does not own us, but he is camped in our territory. In this case, we have to evict him for the healing to come.

I don't like to talk about the enemy; I don't like to give him any glory. But the Lord gave me a picture of a military meeting. I saw a conference in session. It was a military briefing. Here in the United States, it's the Intelligence Department's job to go out and gather information about the enemy. It's their job to figure out where he is, how he works, his tactics and his capability. Then it is the job of this department to brief the other leaders on how the enemy works.

That's what I am going to do now. I am going to give you a military briefing because we are at war. Those who do not understand that we are at war are deceived.

Reflect on what happened to Jesus in the hours before his crucifixion and at the time of his suffering on the cross. Consider the violence of the cross and visualize the violence of which our enemy is capable.

By seeing the violence of the cross, not just as a picture of what Satan intended for Jesus, but as a picture of what he intended for you, you begin to get a glimpse of just how

much Satan hates you. His desire is for your destruction –
he comes to kill, to steal, and to destroy.[79] This is a real live
war, and we are fighting a real live enemy.

I don't say this to scare you, but to wake you up.
Remember, there should be no fear for those of us in the
battle because the Lord Himself fights with us.

Let me comfort all those who may be concerned about
fighting the enemy. Second Samuel 11:1-5 tells the story of
King David and the captain of his armies, Joab. It says,

> *"And it came to pass, after the year expired, at the
> time kings go forth to battle, that David sent Joab."*

What's wrong with this picture? David was a king. It
was the time for kings to go forth to battle. David sent Joab.
David hung around the palace and he sent someone else to
fight the battle that was his to fight. That was verse
one...now read verse two.

> *"And it came to pass in the evening time that David
> arose off from his bed and walked upon the roof in
> the king's house and from the roof he saw a woman
> washing herself and the woman was very beautiful
> to look on."*

You know the rest of the story. David desired the
woman. He did whatever it took to get the woman. He had
her husband, Uriah, killed so that he might have her. And all
this happened because, when it was time for kings to go to
war, David stayed home and he sent Joab.

A little Hebrew lesson for you here; the name Uriah
means "God is my Fire." The name Joab means "Jehovah is
my Father." When Jehovah-is-my-Father goes to war we had
better go too because, if we stay home when we are
supposed to be at war, we may kill the God-is-my-Fire in our

lives. When Father goes to war there is no safer place to be than in the battle because that is where God is. **When God says it's the season for war, the kings don't stay home!**

Who is a king? In the Old Testament, when you conquered territory, you got to be the king of the land you conquered. That's just how it worked. **When you conquer something you have authority over that thing, and you are its king.** You have the power to rule. If you have conquered cancer, you are king over that thing. When God sends the kings to war, that is a call for you to fight. Look for cancer, because you have authority over it. You have the ability to rule over that thing because you have conquered it – it knows your name.

Are you sick? Do you know someone that is sick? That means it's time to go to war, and I am here to give you a briefing on the enemy. I am going to tell you what he looks like and how he operates.

Bondage

Satan is only able to create bondage in your soul with your permission and cooperation. Once he has your agreement, or at least you have decided not to fight him – which is a form of agreement – he enforces that bondage with demonic power. My purpose here is not to get into all the history and theology of demons. Let it be said simply that Jesus found them in people who were called the "the people of God" and He had to kick them out. You will find them today in "the people of God," and you will also have to kick them out.

First, you can't always assume that every problem a person has is because of a demon. Sometimes, it's just our lack of self-control or laziness. Having self-control is hard work. Each one of us is in charge of governing our own soul – our mind, our will, and our emotions. That's a job and a half right there. Each day is filled with new challenges for our souls. Will I lose my temper today? Will I get out of bed at 6:00 a.m. and go to prayer? Will I go one more day without a drink?

For some people, just gaining control of their own desires is a full-time job. Then on top of that, sometimes we end up in a battle for our spiritual lives with the one who wishes to destroy our souls. Often we end up fighting demonic strongholds that have become established in our souls. Sometimes, the first hurdle is to determine if we are fighting a demon or if it's just a matter of getting control of ourselves.

There are some simple clues to look for that will let you know that you are dealing with a demonic spirit and not just a lack of willpower. When I hear phrases like "life-controlling" and "repeated pattern," then I am immediately suspicious. When a person says, "I can't stop myself... I have used all my willpower... I have done everything that I know...I think I am doing fine for a few days, a few weeks, a year or two and then... I am just exhausted fighting this thing because it never goes away," I know I am looking at a demonic spirit.

When the desire causes you to do something that you really don't want to do, or prevents you from doing what you really want to do, it is "life controlling." That is when I am ready to believe that it is probably demonic.

I have met people who despise themselves for looking at pornography, but they cannot stop. I have met people who said, "I really, really wanted to go to that party, but I could not face the possibility that people would not find me likable." When I hear these things, I know I am dealing with something that has control over the person. And I know I am going to do more damage if I say, "Just use your willpower." They can't just use willpower. Something is controlling them. They exhaust themselves; they use all their energy trying to manage their demon, when what they really need is to kick it out.

Listen to the kinds of words that the person says and they will tell you what kind of spirit is operating. A spirit of unbelief says, "You know I really don't believe this process is even going to work. I am not really sure that you can get rid of my demon. I am not sure that I even have a demon. Yes, I know I seem really out of control to the point where I have to be drugged, but I am not sure that I have a demon." Talk about a spirit of unbelief!

It is a demon when the person says that they never really believed they were important, never really worth anything, never believed that they were any good, never believed that they could do anything, did not think they could succeed. They say words like, "I am so lonely. No one really likes me, and even my friends probably just put up with me, and God probably just puts up with me too!" That is a spirit of rejection.

Pay attention to the words. If you start to hear yourself saying these words, STOP. Tell that spirit (and yourself) that you are not going to agree with those lies! Look for those words in the people to whom you are ministering. Look for those words in yourself. Don't let those words into your thoughts and out of your mouth.

When you are dealing with the demonic, you may spot the enemy by observing these clues. Look and listen for things that seem to be in CONTROL of you (or the person to whom you are ministering). Listen for words that help you see how the enemy has gained power.

Some people justify their behavior by saying, "It's just the way that I am. I was born this way. I am stubborn, but I was born this way; it's part of my personality."

Ask these questions: "Is it useful to you? Is it serving you well? Are you getting good results from that attitude or behavior?" When you say that this is who you are and you don't want to change because you are made this way, then I say, "Stay that way, but don't expect your results to change."

It's always amazing to me. Some people will come for help, for counseling, and acknowledge that they are stubborn or jealous. Their marriage is wrecked, their kids don't like them anymore, and they still say things like, "I am just made this way. This is just a part of who I am."

You must be willing to change the things that you think might even be part of your very personality. You have lived with this thing so long, you think, "This is who I am," but it's not!

Let's back up and talk about how the enemy gets so much power in your soul. I mentioned earlier that the power comes from an agreement. This is not a new thought to believers. We have known all along that there is power in agreement. *"If any two of you agree on earth as touching anything...."*[80]

We understand that there is power in the spirit realm when we unite on earth. There is also power given to the enemy in the spirit realm when we unite our souls (our minds, wills, and emotions) with the plans of the enemy. In fact, this is the very source of demonic power.

You cannot just be walking down the street and have a demon jump on you. If you have a demonic spirit operating in your life, you came by it honestly. By that I mean, you spoke a word or took an action that allowed the thing to have power in your life.

I repeat; I don't believe a Christian can be demon possessed. Possession is about ownership, and you have been bought with a price.[81] You have been redeemed. You have been ransomed. But none of you came into this world as a believer. All of you had a life before Christ. In that life, you opened doors of your soul to the one who had plans to destroy you. You opened these doors through the words that you spoke and the actions you took. This caused you to form an agreement, an alliance if you will, with the enemy. Once this agreement was made, the enemy had the right and the power to make it come to pass. **We all come to the kingdom with baggage.**

I think it was Derek Prince who compared the journey of spiritual freedom to the Israelites entering the Promised Land. God had given them the land years earlier. It was theirs for the taking. When they were ready to possess the land they had been promised, God was with them. He made the "getting in" easy. He brought them through the Jordan River by a miracle. The waters parted and they walked across the river.

This is like our born-again experience. We have come into the kingdom, the Promised Land. God brings us from spiritual death into spiritual life by a miracle, an instant act of grace. Yet, although God had given His people the land, it was their job to drive out the enemies. God fought at their side. He gave them the strategy, but they had to take up the sword and confront the enemy themselves. The Lord told them to drive out the enemies. The same is true with the enemies of your soul.

When Israel walked away from Cannan the first time, they chose, by their inaction, to let the enemy live in their land and build buildings and plant crops for forty years. The enemy was quite comfortable there and was not going to leave just because the Israelites had arrived.

I have often thought about this. Why did God make the Israelites fight? Why not another miracle? You can discover the answer by reading the history of Israel. God brought them into the Promised Land by a miracle and then He said, "You see those giants? It is your job to drive them out yourself."

God said that He left the giants there to teach the Israelites how to war.[82] God did not want His people to be victims of their enemies. God allowed Israel to fight the battle, and as long as their ways were pleasing to the Lord, the Lord worked with them to bring the victory.

If you study the battles of Ancient Israel, you will find

that as long as they served God, they were undefeatable. They soon gained a reputation in the land, and most of the wiser nations were afraid to fight them. This allowed them to have a long season of peace in a world where kingdom warring against kingdom was a regular way of life. By allowing them to fight the giants in the land, God established a reputation in His people. They were <u>not</u> victims.

As I said earlier, we all come to the kingdom with baggage. I wish that at the moment we were saved all bondage was dissolved, but that is not the case. God brings us into the kingdom by a miracle. We are justified by faith. It is instant. It is miraculous. We cannot earn it. We could never do it on our own.

But then.... we have to drive out the giants in our own souls. God works with us to give us the victory, but we have to do the actual battle. We are no longer the property of Satan, but because of our past actions and agreements, we have territories of our souls that are still under the influence of the demonic. Our spirits are made alive by faith in Jesus, but our souls need a house cleaning.

We might, for example, be born again, but years later we might still have irrational fear. This is an example of a demonic bondage. To take back control, we have to kick out that spirit of fear and claim back the territory of our souls! This reclaiming of our souls and cleansing them from the giants in the land is the sanctification process. **We are justified by faith; we are sanctified by the life long process of cleaning out our souls.**

Recognizing the enemy is the first step to deliverance and healing. Once you have identified a possible area of bondage in your soul, or the soul of the person to whom you are ministering, the intruder must be cast out.

In the old days of deliverance ministry, we did things the hard way. We did it the way Jesus did it in the New Testament, thinking that was the formula. You will notice that there was often a big bru-ha-ha when Jesus cast out a demon. It was often messy. The demon would throw the person to the ground or there would be some attendant violence. Jesus seemed to allow this behavior and, for years, so did we.

Before I learned what I am about to share with you, I was grabbed and scratched. I had my clothes pulled, and people threw up. Then one day the Lord showed me a vision of what was happening in the spirit realm. (I don't know if this is literal, or it was just a picture He created for me to help me relate to this unseen reality.) I saw an ugly demon with long claws. As soon as the person agreed with whatever lie he was whispering, the demon gained the legal right to sink his claws into the person. Then it was very difficult to dislodge him. When the person renounced the words or actions that formed the agreement, the demon lost his grip. It was as if the person became slippery and there were no hooks for the demon to grab. The demon was still there, hoping the person would change his or her mind and then he could grab hold again, but once the demon let go, then it was easy to say, "Be gone." It would leave with no pain or fuss.

As I meditated on this, it made sense. Words or actions formed an agreement that allowed the demon to attach itself. Undoing that agreement by renouncing the words or actions would remove the legal right for the demon to hold on.

When I changed my method of doing deliverance, it got much easier. People did not go through such pain. After deliverance, they were refreshed, rather than worn out. There were fewer manifestations. Usually people just coughed, burped, or yawned as the demon left.

"Why didn't Jesus do it this way?" you might ask?

I asked that same question myself. As I studied Scripture, it became clear to me that most of what Jesus did was for public viewing. There was no greater show than the casting out of a demon. It was all about a power struggle.

Jesus cast out demons in public to prove that He had power over anything that had power over God's people. He was there to establish His kingdom and demonstrate His superiority in the spirit realm. Jesus <u>wanted</u> a show. It was a sign and wonder to the unbeliever. On the other hand, when we are ministering to someone one on one, there is no need for such a show.

Once you have identified the spirit that needs to be evicted, here is how you go about it. (**Remember, you have looked for clues in the person's speech. Also, you have prayed and asked the Lord what is operating in this situation.**) The Lord will put His finger on something and give you a word of knowledge. Sometimes you will get the actual name of a spirit, but you can name them by their action. You can say, "You spirit that causes her to be afraid of water."

You may get a word of knowledge about the agreement. Many times I will hear the Lord speak an age. If you are ministering to someone else, it is okay to ask confirming questions. For example, let's say you hear the number 15. Then ask the person what happened to them when they were 15 years old that was significant. You can say, "You spirit that came to her at age 15, GET OUT!"

Perhaps you hear the word "idolatry." Most Americans would tell you they have never been involved in idol worship. It's okay to ask questions to pin down the issue. Ask questions like, "Have you ever been part of a false religion where you have prayed to somebody other than God? Have you ever made something in your life so big that you would sacrifice everything for it? Maybe it's your career. You think, "My family will just have to understand. I don't care that I am working eighty hours a week. I don't care that my kids don't know what I look like anymore and my wife is in tears because she has to do everything; it's my career'"

Also, when you are praying for yourself, you will hear the Lord speak a word. **When you hear Him speak something,**

you should assume He knows what He is talking about.
Let's say you hear the Lord speak the word "pride" and you
think, "I don't have any pride; let's see who else You might be
talking to here." Do a little self examination: "Pride? Do I
really? Show me where I missed it. I sure don't want to let the
enemy stay."

You may hear someone preaching and they name a
particular problem or they describe a trap of the enemy, and
all of a sudden you get that Holy Spirit finger poking you in
the stomach. (You know what I am talking about.) You
think, "Oh, that's true of me!" Assume God is right and start
figuring where and when you made an agreement with the
lie of the enemy. Where did it get in? How did it get in?
What was the agreement?

I once ministered to a woman with breast cancer. I told
her that she had made an agreement with a spirit of death.
This shocked her. She had to think about it for awhile. Then
she remembered that she had a thought, which was really a
demonic voice. The thought was this: "Let me put cancer on
you, and then I will heal you."

The voice almost sounded like God because of the
promise of healing. She thought, "I'm really busy now,
maybe later."

Well, later had come. She renounced this agreement and
we commanded healing. When she went back to the doctor,
they checked the tumor again, and it had shrunk consider-
ably in just those few days, with no medical treatment.
Today she is free of cancer, without surgery.

**When you hear a word of knowledge for someone
else, assume you heard correctly even if the person
denies it.** You might be dealing with a lying spirit.

I asked someone in a deliverance session one time,
"Have you ever been molested?" She said no. I knew she
had because that was the word of knowledge I had received.

I gave her a chance to deal with it gracefully. I said, "Let me explain what I meant about "molest." Maybe it isn't what you're thinking I meant." Come at it a different way.

Make it easy for them to open up. Make sure there is no judging or condemning tone in your voice. Remember, these children of God were victims, hostages of the enemy. They fell into a trap. Bondage blocks them from having all the Kingdom benefits God desires for them. Your focus is to find out where the glory of God is blocked in these people. God wants to display His glory in us. We are His creation. We bear His mark. We are bought with a price and He wants to be glorified in us. He wants us free and He wants us healed. **When someone is in bondage emotionally, spiritually, and physically, the question we need to ask is: "What is blocking God's glory in this person?"**

Think for a moment... if a person was able to have the full glory of God displayed in them, what would that look like? What would it look like on this woman? What would be true about her? She would have victory, confidence, freedom... all of these things. So, if you are ministering to someone and they don't look like that, then the glory is blocked. When I am ministering, I ask myself, "What would this person look like if the glory wasn't blocked anywhere in him, and what does it look like now? What is the difference?"

For example, I recognize the spirit of rejection so quickly because there is a closed feeling to the person; that I-am-not-worthy kind of feeling. But I know that's not how Jesus acted. I always use Him as my model because I think He was probably the only one that lived His life completely free of bondage. He said, "*...for the prince of this world cometh, and hath nothing in me.*"[83] So when I see something that does not match the model, I zero in on that place. What is the thing that is causing that discrepancy? **Once God puts His finger on the place where the glory is blocked, break the agreement and kick out the spirit.**

When you are in pain, it's hard to be the one with the

faith. And sometimes lack of faith is the only problem. There are people that have been Christians a long time. They have had many victories in their lives. Chances are that they are not walking around with a load of "baggage" or demonic oppression. They probably have just been in pain so long that it is just hard to believe, and all they need is for you to be the one with the faith.

When you use your faith, and the pain does not go away immediately, it is connected to a pain in the soul. You will not get the person free of physical pain until you deal with the pain in his or her soul.

The enemy is predicable. His methods rarely change. If a person is in spiritual bondage, here is how it happened. The spirit came in at a vulnerable moment in that person's life. There are major junctures, or turning points in each person's life. It might have been a near-death experience because they were in an accident. Maybe it was when their mom told them that they were ugly or criticized them for something. **There is potentially a wound each time a person experiences a strong emotional event in his or her life.** At these moments, there are always two things coming at that person:

There is the grace of God for the moment
and
There is the lie of the enemy.

This happens every time! The age does not matter, and the circumstances do not matter. There is the grace of God that says, "You are beautiful," and, there is the lie of the enemy that says, "Your mom is right; you are really ugly."

At that critical moment you have to decide which thing you are going to believe. Are you going to take the grace of God or the lie of the enemy? For those of you in spiritual or physical pain, I know what choice you made. You took the lie of the enemy.

The enemy came to you with the lie that your mom died at thirty with cancer, your sister died at thirty with cancer, and guess what? Tomorrow you're thirty, you're going to get cancer this year. It is a lie!

So do you take the grace of God which says by His stripes you were healed two thousand years ago? Or, do you take the lie of the enemy, which is attached to fear? Will you say, "I have known this all my life, and now that feeling has come to confirm it and I probably will die this year?"

If you take the lie, then you have just made an agreement with the enemy and it will not be long until you've got yourself some cancer!

That's always how the enemy gets a stronghold-ALWAYS! He has been stripped of his power. All he has left are lies and deception. We must not swallow his lies!

It was my great privilege to hear a sermon by Rev. Terry Law many years ago that changed my life. He spoke about how the enemy has been stripped of his power. He used Colossians 2:15:

"And having spoiled principalities and powers, he made a show of them openly, triumphing over them in it."

The word translated "spoiled" is the Greek word *apekduomai.* The simple definition is *to strip or divest wholly.* Terry Law had diligently researched this word and shared the richness of its meaning. According to him, this was a Roman military term. It was actually the name of a ceremony. When two generals fought a battle, one would win the victory and the other would be defeated. At the end of the battle, the two generals would meet on the battle field. They would be dressed in their full military attire. All of the captains and officers that served under each would also appear on the battle field.

Then the winning general would approach the losing general, and he would begin to strip him of all his rank and titles. He would say, "What was yours is now mine by right of conquest. Whatever lands you held are now mine. Whatever titles you held are now mine. Whatever riches or servants or households you owned are now mine by right of conquest." What a sight it must have been!

General McArthur was the commander of the US forces in the Asian theater during World War II. He was a student of military history. When we won the war against Japan, he required the commander to meet him on a ship in the Pacific. There he conducted an *apekduomai*.

Colossians tells us that on His way back to heaven, Jesus stopped off in the heavenlies and performed an *apekduomai*. The word "triumphing" in that verse means to shout approval and make a procession or parade. Jesus made an absolute spectacle of the enemy. He probably danced and cheered and shouted and noised the event far and wide in the spirit realm. Terry Law paints a picture of what might have taken place that day. Can you imagine Jesus stripping Satan?

"Satan you were called Lucifer, morning star; I am the Bright & Morning Star.

You were called the anointed cherub that covers; I am the Anointed One.

You are called that old serpent; I am the serpent lifted up in the wilderness for the healing of the nation.

You were called an angel of light. I am the Light of the World.

You are called the prince of this world. I am the Prince of Peace, King of Kings.

You were one of the sons of God. I am the Son of God."

Don't miss this point. **Satan lost his power that day.** It is your words and your actions that give Satan his power. He no longer has any of his own power. He has been stripped. The principalities have been spoiled. They have no power, except lies.

You, on the other hand, have tremendous power. The Word says in Mark 11:23, you will have WHATSOEVER you say. Satan has no power, and that is why he wants your power. **If he can get you to agree with him, then you have just given him the use of your power.**

The enemy uses words that may sound familiar. "Ooh, your grandfather had this, and your father had this, and you will get it too." He comes along to deceive you, and the lie comes to you at some tender moment. When you reach out and take the lie, the power is released to bring it to pass. **You "take a lie" by speaking words or taking actions in agreement with the lie.**

Sometimes people remember the first time they agreed with the lie of the enemy. Often they were a child or teenager. They did not know what was happening. When they learn that they swallowed a lie and when they learn that Satan got in that way, they say, "That's not fair."

Satan is not fair. He has no code of ethics. His mission is to steal, kill and destroy, and if he can get you at five years old, all the better. People tell me that they did not know they were making a choice. One of Satan's best plans is to keep you ignorant. If he can keep you ignorant, all the better. Of course, it's not fair. Who said it was going to be fair? That's why we have a champion named Jesus!

When people need deliverance or healing from disease (which is the exact same thing in God's book), I know they have made an agreement with the enemy. How do I know they reached out and took the lie? I know because they are battling illness – otherwise they would be free – but, instead, they are in bondage. Their emotions are messed up. They are taking seven kinds of drugs to try to handle their problems and manage their demons. They have come to be healed because they took the lie.

Please see this: I do not believe that every sickness is a result of personal sin. We live in a sinful, fallen world. We have Chernobyl, acid rain, and pesticides in our food. I believe stuff happens. There was a tower that fell in a town not far from where Jesus ministered. The people asked Jesus about it, as though they had deserved to die for some reason. Jesus answered with words that, today, would be translated, "Stuff happens." He said that they were not any more wicked or deserving of calamity than the rest.[84]

I believe that God knew we would get sick and need healing. Just because you fell and broke your leg does not mean that a demon tripped you. Stuff happens. But the Bible tells us that when stuff happens we should be healed. If you don't have your own faith, go to the elders (who are supposed to have the faith for you).

If you are a believer and you get sick, you should be healed when you follow the instruction to go to the elders. **If you do not recover when the elders pray the prayer of faith, then there is a spiritual issue that must be addressed**. That issue is usually demonic. In that case, there was an agreement made with the enemy. This agreement gave the enemy the right to rule a piece of your soul. That agreement needs to be broken and the enemy cast out!

We are following the healing ministry of Jesus. That means that sometimes, in order to get a cure for cancer, we have to cast out a demon of cancer. **We cannot pick and choose between healing ministry and deliverance ministry.** Look at the mission of Jesus: heal the broken hearted, deliver the captive, and set at liberty them that are bruised.[85] The word "bruised" means "those that had been enfeebled or broken down," used as "I break down."

Obviously, the brokenhearted need healing in the soul. Deliverance was not to those who were in a physical jail, but a spiritual one. Liberty was the remedy for those who were broken.

Did you notice the odd pair of words - Broken vs Liberty? We would normally think of <u>healing</u> those broken, not <u>liberating</u> them. **Jesus lumped healing and deliverance into the same category and called it all healing.**

The description of Jesus ministry is found in Acts 10:38

"How God anointed Jesus of Nazareth with the Holy Spirit and with power: who went about doing good, and healing all that were oppressed of the devil, for God was with him."

The word "oppressed" means "to dominate or exercise lordship over." **Jesus' idea of healing was to end the devil's lordship over someone.**

Jesus also defined deliverance as healing in the story of the Syrophenician woman's daughter who was demon possessed.[86] From this story we get the phrase, "Healing is the children's bread." The bread to which Jesus referred was deliverance.

In Matthew's account of this same story, the author concludes by saying, "the daughter was made whole from that very hour."[87] This word "whole" is the Greek word *"iaomai"* which means "to cure." We can learn much about how the disciples understood Jesus ministry of healing and deliverance by the way they described it to us.

Matthew also used this same word *iaomai* in his story of the centurion's servant who was sick with palsy. Jesus "healed" him.[88] So Matthew used the same word to describe deliverance from a demon and healing from palsy. Matthew chose words that express his understanding - physical healing and spiritual healing (deliverance) are the same.

[72] Luke 13:16

[73] Prince, Derek, They Shall Expel Demons, Chosen Books, Grand Rapids, MI, 1998, 11

[74] Luke 13:12

[75] Mark 2:5

[76] Luke 11:14

[77] John 9:2

[78] Ephesians 4:16

[79] John 10:10

[80] Matthew 18:19

[81] 1 Corinthians 6:20

[82] Judges 3:2

[83] John 14:30

[84] Luke 13:4

[85] Lke 4:18

[86] Mark 7:25-30

[87] Matthew 15:22-28

[88] Matthew 8:13

Breaking the Agreement

Sometimes the person to whom you are ministering will be able to tell you the trigger event that set off the illness. However, in my experience, it is very rare. Usually, I have to ask, using questions based on my experience or get a *rhema* word.

If someone has arthritis, I will ask them about bad relationships and anger. If the woman has breast cancer, I will ask her about her relationships with her mother and sisters. This will get me to the foundation of the problem in about half the time. I also need a word of knowledge. I will write more about that in a later chapter, and I discuss it extensively in my soon to be published book on the theological principles and practical application of prophesy.

For now, just believe, by faith, that when you need to hear from God, He will give you a thought or a clue. You are looking for the name of the spirit/emotion or the trigger event. You can safely assume, every single time, that when the Lord puts His finger on something, it is a factor in the healing.

Cancer is often linked to rebellion or regret. When I ask people with cancer if they were very rebellious in their past, much of the time the answer is yes. Now, I am not talking about a single act of rebellion. I am talking about an agreement with the spirit of rebellion so that it ruled a part of their souls. It became a lifestyle.

When they admit that they could have been the poster child for rebellion, I know that we have found the culprit. I can then tell them the lie that they took. There was the grace of God that said, "Your parents are the covering for you," and there was the lie of the enemy that said, "You should be able to do what you want. You know you are a free person and there is no slavery in America." They bought the lie.

By "buying the lie" I mean that they believed it, put faith in it, and then pretty soon they started speaking it and acting on it. That is when they got in trouble, because then that spirit of rebellion had something to grasp.

Any demonic spirit is able to harness the power of the breath of God in your mouth once an agreement is formed. So, now they're in agreement with the lie of the enemy and now it's operating in their life. That is how it gets in, and that's how it works every single time.

Now, before we got saved, we had a bunch of this spiritual garbage in our souls; some of us had more than others. But the good news is that these demonic forces leave at different times, triggered by certain events in our Christian life. A bunch of them leave when we get saved because they can't hang on beyond the truth of the gospel. The few that can hang on beyond this point can hang on because, even though we get saved, we haven't broken our agreement with them. Demons also leave at baptism. Through baptism, we declare we are dead to the world and we have a new existence in God.

The Rabbis of the Old Testament believed that running (living) water had the ability to separate a person from demonic forces. Before a woman could marry, she had to dip in living water to purify herself spiritually. It was called a *mikvah*, and it was believed to separate her from all those demons of her childhood or generations. This would let her come to the marriage spiritually clean.

In ancient Israel, all the men over the age of 30 had to perform the same type of ritual before the High Holy Days. This was so that they didn't take demons into the Temple with them.[89] In fact, this is what John the Baptist was doing. He was cleansing the men during the time of *Teshuva*, which proceeds the Day of Atonement.

There is scriptural basis for this belief. Numbers 19 talks about the water of separation. If a man touched something dead, he had to be cleansed by the water of separation. It was believed that spirits pass at death and they could transfer to the person who touched the dead body. There are various scriptures that talk about a person having to wash with water after certain actions so that they would be ceremonially clean.[90]

In this way, Scripture instructs that a ceremony of water has the power to separate one from uncleanness. When you are baptized, we believe, by faith, that anything connected with your old life, including demonic powers, is put to death in your life and you are raised to a new life. Why then does it appear that some of the demons "survive" the water?

It is because we take them back. A demon will leave without too much problem when you break your agreement with it. **The problem is rarely getting free; it is staying free.** If you had a spirit of addiction before baptism, then the power of that thing is broken when your old life is buried with Christ. But the voice of your former captor sounds so familiar that soon you speak words and take actions in agreement with that enemy and you return to bondage again, just as quickly as you left it. Sometimes the thing returns so quickly, you think it never left!

The scripture in Ephesians 6 says, "*We wrestle not against flesh and blood but against powers, principalities, rulers of darkness...*"

There are some demonic spirits that only have power to rule in the darkness and, when you bring light into that place, they lose the power to rule. Scripture says you shall know the truth and the truth that you know shall set you free.[91] How can truth set a person free? It can in the spirit realm. When you know the truth, you walk in the light and the rulers of darkness lose their power to rule. This is why, after you are born again, you should attend a good Bible-believing church. You need to be exposed to as much truth as possible. Get free and get built up!

Every once in awhile a spirit will hang on beyond all that. Maybe you have been a Christian for fifteen years, for twenty years, for thirty years. However, you are still dragging that ball and chain along with you. How can this happen? The answer is so simple. You continue to speak words or take actions in agreement with that spirit, and its hold on you is constantly reinforced. At that point, the solution is to kick the thing out. Cast it out!

There are some strongholds, or what we call "strongman" spirits. This simply means that they are the most powerful, longest resident, or most firmly entrenched spirits. In one person it might be a spirit of fear. In another it might be a spirit of rejection.

There is a lot of discussion in the deliverance ministry about strongman spirits and the best way to deal with them. Do you always get the strongman first? Do you wait and get the strongman spirit last after you get all of the other spirits, thus weakening the stronghold?

Here is what I do. I get a *rhema* word. Sometimes I go right for that stronghold and rip it out because that is what I hear the Lord tell me to do.

Sometimes the person cannot even understand what you are saying to them because they are listening through a cloud of demonic chatter. Sometimes you have to speak the truth so that stronghold will begin to weaken. Many times a stronghold is attached to a lying spirit. The spirit of rejection is usually attached to a lying spirit. The spirit of fear is usually attached to a lying spirit. So sometimes I have to go after a lying spirit and get rid of it so that the person can believe the truth. So, contrary to many people who work in deliverance ministry, **I recommend you get a *rhema* about how you are supposed to attack each situation.** God will tell you. It always works, no matter which way I do it, when I do it the way God tells me to do it.

Stronghold are in a person's mind.

> *"(For the weapons of our warfare are not carnal, but mighty through God to the pulling down of **strong holds;**)Casting down **imaginations**, and every high thing that exalts itself against the knowledge of God, and bringing into captivity every **thought** to the obedience of Christ;*[92]

First God tells us that our weapons can pull down strongholds; then He goes on in the next verse to tell us what makes up a stronghold. From this passage, it is plain to see that strongholds are made up of imaginations, and thoughts. This definition should have great implication for people who think spiritual warfare is pulling down strongholds over a city by shouting at demons in the sky. (But, that's another book.)

For now, let's follow this logical path. If strongholds are things we think inside our heads, then it only makes sense that the stronghold can be broken if we deal with the thinking. Thoughts become knowledge and knowledge becomes actions. To break the strongholds, we renounce the words and actions that formed them.

Ministering Deliverance

In deliverance ministry – which is a part of healing

ministry – you must deal with the strongholds of the mind that have kept people believing, and reinforcing, the lie of the enemy. Who knows, there might be ten thousand different demons in the world and I don't even know all of their names. I have found, and others agree, **you can cast out a demon by describing its behavior, without knowing its name**. For example, you can say, "You spirit that causes her to lose her concentration, GET OUT!"

Time and time again I keep running into these same spirits in Christians that cause illness. I have made a list of about seven or eight spirits that keep showing up. Everyone who does deliverance ministry has his or her own list of strongholds and the supporting demons that go with each stronghold spirit. Any good list will do. Use any one you want, or make your own list. I just made a list because I do a particular type of ministry. I am usually focused on getting someone healed. I am not there to deal with every hurt or demonic issue of their life. I am looking specifically for the thing that is connected to the illness. There are ministries that are focused on getting you completely free in all areas of your life. This is usually a five day event.

Deliverance is a simple process. You are simply undoing what the person did to bring the bondage. Interview the person. Ask the person to come prepared to list the things in his or her life that God has put his finger on.

Most believers already know what they need to be delivered from (and we should not do deliverance on unbelievers as a rule), so it makes the job much easier. Also, ask them to briefly discuss any situation that has strong, negative emotions still attached to it. Perhaps someone treated them wrong and they have forgiven them over and over, but when they think about that situation, there is still something operating.

Repent,
Renounce,
Cast Out.

How much more simple could it be? This is the process of deliverance. You are not having them repent for the sin unless they have never repented for the sin. If you are dealing with Christians, this is rarely the case. As a matter of fact, they have probably repented, and repented, and repented and they can't figure out why this thing is still hanging around.

It isn't the sin; God forgave the sin when they repented the first time. Now we are moving down a level. We are moving down to the level of the legal right for the demon to stay. So, we are going to attack it the same way it got in.

Remember, people that need healing and deliverance were faced with a choice. There were two things coming at them at that moment – there was the grace of God and the lie of the enemy. They reached out and took the lie from the hand of the enemy of their God. It is on this point that you focus the repentance. For example, it isn't repenting for thinking of suicide or trying suicide. Believe me, they have repented over and over again. They should repent <u>for receiving the lie of the enemy</u> that said suicide was the solution to their problem and for believing that it was the way out.

They made an agreement with that lie. They probably even spoke words like, "I hate myself. I wish I were dead." They must repent of opening the door to this thing, inviting it in, receiving the lie, coming into agreement with it. Get them to renounce their words and action and break their agreement with that spirit. There is a difference between repenting for the sin and the kind of repentance that we are doing. We are getting at a very deep level, a legalistic level, because demons are very legalistic.

Begin by looking for evidence of demonic opportunity.

Obviously, you are looking for both entry points and spirits. (Shortly, I will give you a starter list of doors and spirits).The Holy Spirit will give you a picture or word about where the enemy has a grip. It takes a bit of practice to focus your search. If you are trying to get a person free of all bondage, then just deal with whatever comes up. If you are trying to get someone healed, you probably don't have to deal with some issues. A spirit of lust probably has nothing to do with a person's injured knee.

When the Holy Spirit puts His finger on something, deal with it simply. Tell the person that you don't need to know the whole story, although most will want to tell it. If the story is graphic (sexual or violent) do not let them tell you the details. It will create a mental image in your mind that you will then have to fight off.

If you are praying for someone at the altar, you may only have a few minutes to get a word, cast out a spirit, command the healing and thank God for the recovery. This is a very difficult situation. Although I have prayed for people that have been healed in 15 or 20 minutes, it is rare. Generally, the things that have brought them into bondage have built up over decades and it often takes and hour or two to get a person healed.

It is best if you can set aside time to get to all the roots of the issue. This gives you the opportunity to instruct them how to stay free. If you have the luxury of an hour or more, make some notes as you are ministering. As the person speaks, make a list of the potential spirits that could be operating. My training has been, when in doubt, cast it out. Also make a list of what I call "collateral spirits." Some spirits travel in groups. For example, lust always comes attached to a spirit of divination. If a person has ever been involved in the occult, you have to cast out all the sexual spirits also. A spirit of doubt attaches to a lying spirit. Tell people that you will no doubt cast out some things that are not there, but it does no harm to cast out a spirit that is not there.

Hand them the list you have made. Many times they are surprised to see what you have put on the list. Ask them to start at the top and repent and renounce each item on the list. Remind them that this is not about the sin. God has forgiven the sin. This is about breaking the legal agreement for the spirit to rule.

There is really a dual thing happening in most cases. For example, someone steals money and repents of stealing the money, and that's where most people stop. What I am saying is that they also made an agreement with the lie of the enemy that they were justified in carrying out the action of stealing. **That action will repeat if they do not get to the root of the matter**. Stealing was a sin, but the root sin was swallowing the lie of the enemy that it was OK to do it.

Sometimes it seems hard to accept the fact that they should repent when they were the victim. I use the example of the woman who was raped and became bitter. She needed to repent of having believed the lie of the enemy, which said that God did not take care of her. Then she needed to renounce having received this lie as a sin. I do this so that they clearly see how the enemy worked in the situation. The fact that swallowing the lie was a sin is usually a revelation to people.

Once again, here is the picture of how a spirit got in. At the time of a trauma or offense, there were two things coming at a person. There was the grace of God for that situation, and there was the lie of the enemy. At that critical moment, the person reached out and took the lie. I know this is true because here we are 10 years later still discussing it. When the person accepted that lie, he or she formed an agreement with it by speaking the lie. This gave that spirit power in the person's life. The repentance then is centered on removing the legal right for the spirit to hold on. Repentance sounds like this:

I repent of opening the door to the spirit of fear and giving that thing access to my life by believing the lie of the enemy. I repent for letting this spirit have control over my life and using me for its own purposes. I renounce any words I have spoken or actions I have taken in agreement with it. I break my agreement with the spirit of fear.

Once they have truly repented, use the scripture in John 20:23 to **declare that the sins have been remitted.** We know that spirits attach to sin, but I have found that spirits will attach to the lie that the sins are not forgiven. Use the authority that Jesus gave the believers whom He sent out. Quote the scripture, and look them square in the eye and say, "Based on your repentance, I use the authority delegated to me by Jesus and I declare those sins remitted."

Obviously, only God forgives sin. According to the dictionary, the word "remit" means "to transmit the payment, to refrain from exacting a tax or penalty, to cancel, to pardon or forgive, to restore to a former condition or position; to refer to another court for further consideration or action." So, we have the authority to declare these things done on earth because the Lord has done them in heaven.

Declare this to them and tell them, "You are eternally separated from these sins, and I declare they can no longer be held to your account. I forbid the enemy from extracting a penalty from you based on prior bad acts. I break the recompense of past sins and declare that you shall not eat the fruit of it."

I have found this declaration of sins remitted to be an extremely powerful tool in deliverance. I have seen people delivered the moment I speak these words.

The next job is to cast out and plant. Explain to the person what will take place as you cast these spirits out. Speak with a firm voice. The spirits do not know what is in your heart. Only God knows the heart of man. Spirits only know what is in your heart or mind when you speak or take some action, so **speak in a manner that is meant to convey a strong knowledge that you know they must go.** Screaming at demons is not necessary. Just be firm.

When Jesus addressed these spirits, Scriptures say that He used a harsh rebuke. There are two terms used in these situations. The first is "cast out," when means "to eject." The second is "rebuke" which means "to forbid."

I also explain to people they will be able to notice a difference once the spirit leaves. Before being cast out, the spirits will feel like they are right inside their head or inside their chest (A spirit of death will manifest in the belly.) Once the spirits are cast out, they will seem to be on the outside speaking in, rather than on the inside speaking out.

Once the legal rights are broken through the person's repenting and renouncing, take the list and, one by one, cast out the spirits, "in the name of Jesus and by the power of the Holy Spirit." I like to use some terms I learned from Peter Horrobin such as, "In the name of Jesus of Nazareth that came in the flesh." (Because the demons have no flesh and that's why they want yours.)[93] There are some other phrases like this that I use, and I have seen success each time. Send the spirits to the dry places because Jesus said that's where they go.[94] At this time also break any word curses, generational curses or soul ties that have been revealed.

As I mentioned earlier, we generally don't do this type of ministry for unsaved people. This is mostly because the person receiving ministry has to do the hard work of staying free. This means replacing the lies they have believed with the truth from the Word, on an ongoing basis. When I cast out something, I try to remember a scripture that speaks of the opposite aspect of God. If, for example, I cast out fear, I plant a sound mind.[95]

If possible, you should give them the Word of the Lord

that is the opposite of the lies that the enemy has told them. Warn them that the spirits <u>will</u> return to see if they can get back in and they have a short time to become familiar with the applicable scripture verses that refute the lies they have previously believed. Remind them that Jesus had every weapon of the universe at His disposal, and His weapon of choice when Satan came was the Word, the same weapon we have. This is also the time for them to use the term "rebuke." Once these spirits are on the outside of them, they must rebuke them, and then the spirits will leave.

After you are finished casting out, ask the person to review the list and tell you if all the spirits are gone. By this I mean, are they on the outside? If the answer is yes, proceed. If not, go back to the spirits that have hung on and dig deeper.

Pray for the discernment of the name of the spirit. I ask questions like, "When did you first experience this?" I tell them that we will keep going until they are free. I say this for the confidence of the person and the fear of the spirit. One of the big battles that people face when they come for deliverance is with the spirit of unbelief. This spirit tells them that it won't work for them.

Once a person tells me they are free, I give them the list I have made and tell them to tie it around a rock and take it to the river or ocean and throw it in. When they do, they are to ask the Lord to forever separate them from these things and receive these things into His Sea of Forgetfulness. I tell them that if the enemy comes back with this junk, they are to remember that they are eternally separated from these things.

Having them throw the list in the water is a modern day way of building an altar. In Old Testament times, when God did something notable for His people, they would build an altar. It was a physical reminder of the hand of God in their lives. Throwing away the list of the things that bound a person has the same effect. They can point back to that day they threw the list in the water and declare that it has left them. Just like the building of the altar, it is a way to take an action that reflects the feelings in the soul.

Here is a list of some of the most common issues/spirits with which I have dealt over the years. It is by no means comprehensive. Consider it a way to prime your discernment pump. You are trying to discover if <u>at anytime in their lives</u> they have ever experienced or been involved in any of these things. Most people discount things that they did before they got saved. You have to say, "At any time in your life have you been involved in or have you experienced..."

➤ **Victim of Violence or Abuse** – hatred, murder, fear, anger, death, rage, retaliation, resentment, suicide, abortion.

➤ **Fear** - traumatic experience, phobias, hysteria, near death (this should be tailored to the actual event that caused the trauma.)

➤ **Rejection** – self hatred, fear of man, fear of failure, lying spirit, insecurity, inferiority, self-pity, loneliness, inadequacy, ineptness, shyness, persecution, paranoid, despair, depression, defeatism, hopelessness, discouragement

  • can manifest as opposite spirits of: pride, judging, criticism, faultfinding, arrogance.

➤ **The Occult /Witchcraft**
  • **Divination** in all forms including Ouija boards, tarot cards, transcendental meditation, crystal balls, palm reading, horoscopes, psychics, etc. (you will find something in this category if they

tell you they have a problem hearing the voice of God.)
- **Sorcery** (the acts of the occult) idolatry, manipulation, magic, incantation, charms, fetishes, drugs, deception, control, word curses, covenants
- **Rebellion** – (parents, teacher, boss, spouse) self-will, stubbornness, disobedience, pride.

➤ **Sexual Sin and Soul Ties** – pornography, homosexuality, rape, incest, bondage, bestiality, prostitution, fantasy, masturbation, molestation, adultery, fornication, bondage, lust (whenever you find a spirit of lust, you will find a spirit of witchcraft. In fact, I usually ask about the Occult question first and if they answer yes to anything in that category, I tell them that I also know that they fight a spirit of lust because these two hang out together. This takes the pressure off them to admit a spirit of lust.)

➤ **Generational Curses** - alcohol, drugs, or any addiction such as gambling, health problems, learning problems, fears, poverty, gluttony, compulsive, mental illness, adultery, "bad luck".

➤ **False Religions/cults** – worship of Mary for Catholics, Islam, Buddhism, Taoism, Hinduism, Shintoism, Confucianism, Jehovah's Witness, Christian Science, Rosicrucianism, Mormonism, Bahaism, etc. This category would also include anything that they put before God. Also Masons, cults, secret societies such as sororities or fraternities where they swore oaths.

➤ **Unforgiveness** – Go all the way back to childhood, parents, teachers etc., also, anyone who might have embarrassed them or let them down. This could even include a parent who died early and "left" them.

Now, I am going to describe how I usually deal with these very common issues/spirits. Please let it be a pattern for how to deal with all spirits.

Let's say the first one I confront is **Abuse.** This can mean that the person was a victim of abuse or violence. It does not necessarily mean sexual abuse, but it can be. Or, it might be that they were an abuser.

In deliverance ministry, we have discovered that spirits like to nest together. Have you have wondered where the term "kindred spirits" come from? Kindred spirits are spirits that are similar and like to hang out together. One may open the door and both will come in. A spirit of hatred, for example, has an affinity with spirits of murder, anger, death, rage, retaliation, resentment, and suicide. These can all attach to a spirit of abuse or violence. One gets in and digs in real deep, and then it holds the door open for its buddies.

If you find somebody that has been a victim of violence, then probably they have had thoughts of suicide. You can tell which demons are operating by the thoughts that the person has. It doesn't always mean that they have that demon, but they may. For sure, if they are having thoughts of suicide, then that demon thinks that there is a way in, and it's hanging around looking to see if it can get the person to agree with it. So, if they are having that thought, then there is a demon of suicide hanging around. **When in doubt, cast it out.**

Maybe they were a victim of violence and the spirit of violence keeps hoping to get them to agree with it. For men, usually the agreement finds external expression. They will commit an act of violence. For women, that spirit of violence usually finds an inward expression. They will begin to do violence to themselves through self-destructive thoughts and behaviors.

When you find one of these spirits, look to see what else might have attached to it. You can ask questions like, "Did you ever think about murdering anybody? Do you lose your temper? Do you fly into a fit of rage?" If the answer is yes, you know there are kindred spirits present.

Fear can come in at any point. Traumatic experiences are a common entry point for fear. The event produces fears, phobias, and hysteria. Near-death experiences are a huge entry point. Perhaps the person was in an auto accident and he or she almost died. It is possible for a spirit of death or fear of death to have come in at that point. All it takes is for the person to say something like, "I should have died." Usually when there is fear of one type, it holds open the door for other fears as well. If they have a fear of death, they may also have a fear of insufficiency, or fear of failure or claustrophobia

Another stronghold spirit is **Rejection**. You will find this in both men and women, but more so in women. Probably 75% of the women to whom I have ministered have had a spirit of rejection. All autoimmune diseases have a link to the spirit of rejection. You must get the person delivered from rejection in order to get them healed of something like fibromyalgia.

Now I am going to tell you something that I know is true from experience. I can't tell you why it works; I just know it does. When dealing with a spirit of rejection, extra steps are usually required. Ephesians 6:12 says, *"We wrestle not against flesh and blood but against powers, principalities, rulers of darkness....."*

One expert in this field taught me that there are some spirits that only have power to rule in the darkness. When exposed to the light (the truth), they lose their power to rule.

In John 8:32 Jesus says, *"And you shall know the truth, and the truth (that you know) shall make you free."* Jesus was talking to believers about the bondage that sin brings, and He revealed a powerful tool for setting the captives free – truth. Rejection, for example, seems to be one of those spirits that can only rule in darkness. It is very vulnerable to the light (truth). This spirit never works alone; it is always attached to a lying spirit. You must deal with both.

The traditional approach (repenting and renouncing) is rarely sufficient to deal with a spirit of rejection if it has become deeply entrenched. Subjecting it to truth ALWAYS works. When a spirit of rejection has successfully operated in someone for a long time, the result is that the person begins to feel rejected by God as well. This is the place to attack this lie.

Tell people who are under a spirit of rejection to turn all their thinking and judging off and just listen to you speak some truth to their spirits. Talk to them about how much God loves them. Gently weave in the gospel message, since it is the power of God unto salvation (*sozo* – the whole package which includes deliverance). Talk about how God created them as unique individuals with unique voice prints, and God can pick out their voices among the millions. Use scriptures like Psalm 139 and put it in the first person, as though God were speaking it to them.

"I have searched you and I have known you ...I have encompassed your path ... where can you go from My presence...If you ascend up into heaven, I am there: if you make your bed in hell, behold, I am there. If you take the wings of the morning, and dwell in the uttermost parts of the sea; Even there shall My hand lead you, and My right hand shall hold you. If you say, Surely the darkness shall cover me; even the night shall be light about you...How great are My thoughts toward you; if you could count them, they would be more than the grains of sand on the earth..."

When you hit a point where you feel the anointing of God, "dig in" at that point. Let God prophetically give you the words to expand the thought. For example, "On those days when you made your bed in hell, when you thought that I had left you and you felt all alone, I was there. When you determined to make your bed in hell, the Lord said, 'Then I guess we shall both sleep in hell tonight, because I will never leave you.'"

I also use Romans 8:35, 38, 39

> *"Who shall separate us from the love of Christ? Shall tribulation, or distress, or persecution, or famine, or nakedness, or peril, or sword? For I am persuaded, that neither death, nor life, nor angels, nor principalities, nor powers, nor things present, nor things to come, Nor height, nor depth, nor any other creature, shall be able to separate us from the love of God, which is in Christ Jesus our Lord."*

Speak about the awesome price that God paid through Jesus so they could have access to God; the love of God that knew no price to great to bring them back into fellowship. After about five minutes of speaking these truths, you will be able to see that the truth has done its job. The person probably will be crying, and you will sense they are ready to reject the lie they have believed for so long. This is the time to gently ask them to reject that spirit of rejection and the lies that have come with it. You will find that it is now easy to dislodge. The truth has set them free! **If you want to be good at healing, you must learn how to deal with this spirit.**

Another category of stronghold spirits is **Divination.** The way I define divination is this: seeking to get information in the spirit realm from a source other than God. It is horoscopes, tarot cards, Ouija boards, psychic hotlines, palm reading, crystal balls, etc. All these things are divination.

One day I heard the Lord speak to me out of the clear blue. I heard the Lord say that divination was the original sin. I started to argue with him.

"No, the original sin was rebellion," I thought.

Then I considered it again. If divination is seeking to get information in the spirit realm from a source other than God, it began to make sense.

The serpent came to Eve and said, "If you eat this fruit, you will <u>know what God knows</u>." Eve turned away from God as her source of information and she looked to another source. It eventually shut down the voice of God in her life.

That's what divination will do for you. It shuts down the voice of God in your life. When you look to some source other than God for your spiritual information, your spiritual hearing is blocked.

Whenever we have students in our prophetic schools who just can't hear God, we immediately know what is wrong with them. So we ask them, "Have you, at any time in your life, ever touched divination?" If so, that spirit is probably still hanging on, so we kick it out.

The other thing that shuts down the voice of God in your life is **Rebellion.** We find this in the life of Saul. When he rebelled, he couldn't get a word from God through all the normal ways. It drove him to a witch.

On this topic, there is a trilogy of spirits that have formed a union. When you find one, you will find the others. We believe the union goes back to the time of the temple prostitutes. Men would come to the oracles (temples of false gods) for a word or to worship. As part of the ceremony, the prostitutes would give the men hallucinogenic drugs to heighten the pleasure of the experience with them. As a result, we find **drugs and lust and divination all hang out together.** When you find one, you have to kick out the others.

Sexual Sins and Soul Ties are very common. Almost always, the entry point for a sexual sin was pornography. I have found that this entry point is so common that I have stopped asking people if they have ever looked at pornography. Instead, I have started asking them, "At what age did you first encounter pornography?"

Actually, I don't care so much about the age; the question gets the focus off of the fact that they did it, and more to the point of when it happened. I have only had one person catch me, and he was an attorney. After I asked the question, he opened his mouth to answer and then said, "Hey wait a minute. I never told you that I ever looked at pornography."

I asked, "Well, have you?" and he answered, "Yes."

Notice also that I used the word "encounter." It takes the blame off them. Maybe a friend gave them the magazine, and by the time they opened the pages to see what it was, the image had already registered. It is also easier for people to ease into a discussion of sexual issues if you soften it in this way. It may help you to be less judgmental when dealing with people if you remember that they are the victims of a demonic plot to entrap them.

So pornography is almost always the entry point for sexual sins. Sometimes, if the person was sexually abused in his or her childhood, that may be the entry point. As a side note, if the person answers "yes" to any question in the witchcraft category, then you know he or she has a spirit of lust. **A spirit of lust and a spirit of witchcraft hang out together.** They're best buddies, and you will never find one without the other. So, if the person has ever touched witchcraft, kick out a spirit of lust also.

One of these spirits, like lust, gets in and develops a stronghold. It is usually pornography, who then holds the door open for the rest of them. That spirit of lust says to the person, "Wouldn't you like to try what you saw?" And when the person does, it says to that person, "You know, now, that's not enough. Wouldn't you like to try something else and something else and something else?" And the person ends up in total sexual bondage.

I hurt for those people who sit across from me in a deliverance session when it dawns on them that looking at pornography at the age of fifteen allowed the spirit of adultery to have access to them and that is why their marriage is wrecked now.

That person will usually say, "Why didn't anybody tell me? My life is down the tubes, my marriage is in a wreck, I am about to lose my job, and you're telling me it started when I was fifteen years old and when I looked at a <u>Playboy</u> magazine?"

Sadly, that's how it happened. When I speak to youth groups, I try to warn them and tell them that's how these things get in. They may lie dormant for years. Then one day they rise up and you find yourself with major sexual addiction, sexual sin, lack of faithfulness and all sorts of stuff.

The really bad news is that you bring that into your marriage. Let's say the young man looks at the <u>Playboy</u> magazine. It causes him to seek the opportunity to try what he has seen. So, he commits fornication, which is sex outside of marriage. Maybe he gets into some other stuff as well. Now, he is married and he and his wife become one flesh. **She is now exposed to all that spiritual garbage because demonic spirits pass along the lines of soul ties.** If you are wondering why you are having some problems being one flesh with your mate, it might be because you brought spiritual garbage along with you, and your spouse is repelled by it.

There are natural, good, holy soul ties like that between a father and a son, or a husband and wife. Those are good, normal healthy soul ties created by God. But we are capable, with our free will, of creating soul ties that were never of God. We also may pollute the ones that were of God.

If you have sex with someone, or become emotionally one with them, you create a soul tie. This means you get a piece of somebody else's soul and they get a piece of yours. The scriptural reference for this is Genesis 34:3. Shechem raped Jacob's daughter, Dinah. The Scripture says, "*And his soul clave unto Dinah...*" The word "clave" is the Hebrew word *dabaq* and it means to cling or adhere to.

Imagine two colored pieces of construction paper glued together; one yellow and one purple. After the glue has dried, if you try to separate them, little pieces of one paper will end up on the other and vice versa. This is the way it is in the spirit realm. If you make a soul tie with someone, then that person is walking around with a piece of your soul.

Sex is not the only way to make a soul tie. Back in junior high school we girls used to prick our fingers and mix our blood to become blood sisters. That, too, can be an unholy alliance. No matter whether it is a good soul tie or a bad one, no matter how you made it, demons can pass along the lines of soul ties. So the soul tie you have can be an open channel for the demonic.

It is important to break those unholy soul ties, but there is a part of this process people sometimes leave out. If you have only broken your soul ties, then all you have done is stop the flow of demonic activity. This is good, but not complete. Remember, there are still people walking around out there with pieces of your soul clinging to them. You need to release the parts of the souls that have clung to you and **call back** the parts of your soul that have clung to another, and pray that God would make you whole again.

There was a woman who started having dreams of having sex with other men years after she was married. These men were not men that she recognized. She would wake up feeling so sinful and dirty. She would repent, in case there was anything in her that could be causing this. During the day, she had no problems with her thoughts. She was completely in love with, devoted to, and faithful to her husband. Why the dreams?

She told a friend about this and the friend recommended she pray before going to sleep. This did not change anything. Then she visited a prophetic conference. A prophet gave her a word that she needed to break her soul ties. She broke all her soul ties, and the dreams stopped that same day. She has never had one since. Those people were out there sinning with a piece of her soul and it was affecting her.

I attended a special workshop on deliverance for sexual bondages. The instructor told us this story. She was doing deliverance on "Mary," who had been involved in a sexual relationship with "John." She broke the soul tie. Then she released any part of John's soul that had clung to Mary and called back any part of Mary's soul that had clung to John. As she said these words, both she and Mary saw an image of Mary walk into the room and step inside of Mary. They did not see it "in the spirit." They saw it with their own eyes! I have done this for so many people. I have people tell me that after we break the soul ties and ask God to take all the pieces and make them whole again, they feel complete for the first time in years.

I know that some will think this strange, but I take the breaking of soul ties one step further. Leviticus 17:11 says that the life is in the blood. The word for "life" in this verse is the Hebrew word *nephesh.* It comes from the word *naphash,* which means to breathe. The word *nephesh* is most often translated "soul."

You can find examples of this translation in Genesis 2:7. God breathed life into man and man became a living *nephesh.* Another use of this word is found in Genesis 34:3 in the story of the rape of Dinah. Shechem's *nephesh* clung to Dinah. So the verse in Leviticus 17:11 could have appropriately been translated, "The soul is in the blood." For this reason, when I am breaking soul-ties, **I break the soul ties that might have come as a result of blood transfusions.**

Here is how you might pray that kind of prayer:

167

> *In the name of Jesus, and by the power of the Holy*
> *Spirit, every unholy alliance that I have made with*
> *my body or has come to me as a result of sharing*
> *blood, I break that soul tie now. I release the part of*
> *other's souls that have clung to me and I call back*
> *any part of my soul that has clung to others. God, I*
> *ask that you make me whole again.*

Generational Curses are very common among believers. What issues do you see repeated from generation to generation? Is there alcoholism? Is there poverty? Is there disease? If they tell you alcoholism or heavy use of tobacco runs in their families, it is a spirit of addiction that has come down the generational lines. So don't treat it like cigarettes. Treat it like an addiction. If all you do is solve the problem of cigarettes, then tomorrow they will gain fifteen pounds because then they may become addicted to food. That spirit just changes clothing.

I probably deal with generational spirits a bit differently than you have been taught in the past. A generational spirit is a familiar spirit. It is a spirit that hangs around you during your life time. It knows all about you. It knows your favorite color and what you ate for breakfast.

Familiar spirits like to hang around families. When your father dies, that spirit tries to come to you. It knows you, it knows your family and wants to stick around. However, spirits cannot just jump on you. There has to be a door that is open. You can open that door with your agreement. Remember, an agreement is formed by words or actions.

Maybe your father always lost his temper. That spirit of anger will come to you. If you get angry and lose your temper, then you have taken an action in agreement with it. Every male in your family may have been an alcoholic, but you will never be one unless you take a drink. Every woman in your family may have died at the age of 40 from breast cancer, but you won't unless you enter into an agreement with the spirits that caused it. When I do deliverance for generational issues, I have people repent for agreeing with the familiar spirits and renounce their words or actions that opened the door. Then I kick it out.

Another common stronghold is **False Religions** – worship of something other than God. This might be praying to saints and Mary, being a part of the Masons, being a part of a secret society, or joining fraternities or sororities where you took a pledge or made an oath. I have never heard of a sorority or fraternity that did not have something in the oath that could be a potential problem. Even saying that you pledge your oath to the sorority or fraternity may take your allegiance away from God.

Unforgiveness will absolutely block healing. That is a big one! The Bible says that we must forgive in order to be forgiven.[96]

One time I was going down a list with a lady and we were casting out a bunch of stuff. One of the things that she had on her list was unforgiveness. She had a teacher in eighth grade who had embarrassed her in front of the class, and she really just had a hard time forgiving her all these years.

I repeated the statement I always make: "There were two things coming at you at that time because it was a big emotional event in your life. There was the grace of God which said, 'The teacher just doesn't know any better. Give that wound to Me and let Me heal it.' Then there was the lie of the enemy which said, 'You have been wronged, you have been shamed, you should have unforgiveness, you should never forgive that woman for what she did for you. That was so awful! Nobody should treat you like that... blah, blah, blah, blah.'" She took the lie of the enemy. I knew this because there was still lots of emotion attached to this event.

I had her repent of all this stuff. After she repented, I

kicked out all the demons, but when I got to this one, it would not leave. I asked her, "What are you holding on to?"

She said, "I don't know."

I asked the demon, "What is you legal right to stay?"

The demon answered, "She didn't mean her repentance."

I looked at the lady and asked her if that was true. She blurted out, "I just don't see how it was my fault!"

"Okay, let's start over here. There were two things coming at you...."

Once she truly repented, the power was broken and she was set free.

Can you cast out a demon if the person does not repent and renounce? Absolutely, yes! It is harder work, and it can be messy. If you will persist, and you are willing to put up with whatever it takes, you can kick a demon out without the person repenting.

Maybe I am kind of lazy, but I just don't like to work that hard. Also, why should I work so hard to get someone free when that person won't help? I also consider it unwise to do so. First, if a person does not want it out, how long do you think it will stay out? Not long! **By taking the person through the steps of repenting and renouncing, I make that person take ownership of his or her own deliverance.** It is much easier for people to understand what got them in the mess and how to stay out of it in the future if I walk them through the process.

If the demon is not going out, one of two things is happening – they didn't mean their repentance, or it's hanging on to something else. For example, the spirit of suicide might be attached to a spirit of abortion. Both are murdering spirits. When people take part in their own deliverance by repenting and renouncing the agreement, the deliverance is very easy. You just say, "Get out!" and the demons leave.

When they won't repent, the spirits sometimes tear at

them. In those cases, I have had people throw up or say, "Oh, that hurts, that hurts!" I have had some other really nasty stuff happen. I've been grabbed, scratched, and all sorts of things. I have now decided that if some people don't want to be free enough to repent, they can just keep all their demons.

There is an exception. When people are demon possessed and their minds are so gone that they can't even agree with you, they can't participate. In that case, bind the mind-controlling spirit. You can kick it out without their agreement and without their permission because you have the same Holy Spirit Jesus had.

Here is the problem. If they don't want that demon out, they are not going to do what it takes to keep it out. Getting the demon out is the easy part. The hard part is keeping it out! Chances are that the spirit has been there for some time and was quite comfortable. It will be back, probably within 24-48 hours. You have only this much time to minister to these people in order to prepare them to resist the enemy. That spirit will return and say something like, "It didn't work. I am still here. You will never be free."

Fortunately, we have learned the enemy's tactics. There is a way for people to know that the deliverance was successful, and that this voice is a lie. Before the deliverance session, they had strong emotions or thoughts. These emotions were the product of demonic thoughts that had taken hold on the inside of the soul. These emotions were so strong that they seemed to well up inside and rise up into the throat. They might have created a tightness in the chest, making it difficult to take a deep breath.

After deliverance, there will be a noticeable difference. The enemy's words will sound exactly the same. The thoughts will be the same. But now it will seem that the thought is coming at their heads from the outside, like a thought that it trying to get back in. There will now be little or no emotion attached to the thought. Before deliverance, that thought was so engrained that it felt like it was the person's own thought. It felt like it was part of them. After deliverance, when they hear that voice again, they will think, "Where did that come from?"

Tell them this is a critical moment. When that voice returns, they are not to entertain it. Do not pet it. Do not agree with it. Turn on it like it was a mad dog and say, "You spirit of rejection, you are not getting back into this body! I rebuke you in the name of Jesus! I am free of you, because Jesus set me free! Praise His name!"

That is how you stay free. It takes some work. If some people won't even agree to repent and renounce, how are they going to do the hard work of staying free? You are better off to leave them with all of their demons. Jesus told us that when we kick out a demon, it comes back. If there is nothing in its place to keep it out, it finds the place clean and swept. It will come back in with seven of its kind more evil than itself and the latter condition of the man will be worse than the former one.[97]

After you have done deliverance, take just a few minutes to plant something good in the place of what you have just kicked out. Get yourself a couple of good scriptures and give those people something to fill the empty place. Talk to them about the voices that will come back and teach them what to do. Tell them to rebuke that spirit in the name of Jesus. They are not to entertain it. At the end of this book I have included a couple of pages on "How To Keep Your Deliverance." Feel free to use it liberally.

By now you are asking yourself, "I wonder if I can do deliverance on myself?" The answer is yes. Use this same process and it will work. The problem is that many times we do not recognize the work of the enemy in our own lives. We all have blind spots. But, if you recognize it, break your agreement and kick it out.

Now, all this may sound like a lot of work. It is certainly

much longer than what Jesus did. You can do it Jesus' way; no repenting and no renouncing. There will most likely be a demonic manifestation, just as when Jesus did it.

The better you get at hearing the *rhema* word, the less time it will take. I have prayed for a person, gotten the name of one spirit, and had the person renounce and then kick it out. The person was immediately healed. The whole thing took 15 minutes. Oh, that they were all so simple. I believe that, as we all get better at hearing the *rhema*, healings will come quicker. Jesus had perfected this skill. He never even spoke a word unless He heard the Father say it.

---

[89] Berthelson, Lou., "Holiness for these Awesome Days" Destiny Image Publishers, Shippensburg PA, 1991, 85-86

[90] Leviticus 11, 15, 17, 22

[91] John 8:32

[92] 2 Corinthians 10:4-5

[93] Horrobin, Peter, "Healing Through Deliverance", Sovereign World Ltd., Kent, England, 1994, 252-253

[94] Luke 11:24

[95] 2 Timothy 1:7

[96] Matthew 6:14-15

[97] Luke 11:26

Body-Soul Connection

**Whatever you allow in
your soul will eventually
manifest in your body**

The connection between the body and the soul is a well documented medical fact. If you worry, you get ulcers. Stress can cause a heart attack. The truth is that we are still discovering connections all the time.

When I conduct healing classes, I usually take someone out of the audience and get that person healed in front of everyone as a demonstration. While doing a healing conference in a church in New York I ministered to a woman with lymphedema. The lymph system is responsible for transporting waste material to the veins. The veins deliver the waste to the other organs which are responsible for the whole waste disposal process of your body.

The lymph node under her arm was no longer working. Her arm was extremely swollen as a result. The arm was in such bad shape that she had it taped to her body so that it could not move. Furthermore, she could not lift her arm. If she did, it came out of the socket. She was on prescription medication for the pain and it was not effectively relieving the pain. Do you have the picture? The woman was in agony.

As I prayed for a word of knowledge, I kept hearing the Lord say, "What you see in her body is a manifestation of what is going on in her soul." Over and over again I heard these words.

This was not the way I usually heard the Lord speak to me during a healing session. Usually he just told me the thing that was blocking the healing and I would cast it out. This time, He was trying to teach me about the relationships between the soul and sickness. Frankly, at the moment, in front of all those people, I was just wishing He would give me the answer. Now I am so glad He didn't because I learned something very valuable.

Back to the story. I thought through what I knew about this illness. By the way, if you don't know the details of an illness, the sick person can always tell you because they know it in great detail. In this case, I already knew that the illness blocked the disposal of waste. So, I tried to make a correlation to the soulish realm. I figured she had some bad thoughts or feelings that she was holding in.

In my mind, I saw a picture of a fence that blocked things from getting out. Then the word "offense" came to me. That made sense. An offense would be a bad emotion. (Many times God uses word plays with me.) That night I had about 200 people watching me stand there in silence as I work through this. Thank God I didn't care that it looked like I did not know what I was doing! I learned a lesson that night that has brought healing to multitudes.

I said to the woman, "Has someone offended you and hurt you emotionally and are you keeping that bottled up inside?" She admitted that this was true. Then I asked her if the symptoms of this disease started after the offense, and again she said that this was true.

From that point it was simple. I had her repent for taking offense. I had her renounce her agreement with the spirit of offense. I cast out that spirit and commanded her lymph gland to function. We started thanking God for her healing. As we were doing that, she said that the pain left. She wanted to un-tape her arm. I left the decision up to her. She did un-tape it and was able to lift her arm with no problem. I saw this woman two days later and her arm was completely healed. All the swelling was gone and her arm was the same size as the other one. Praise God!

This story gives me the opportunity to say that as the minister, you should never recommend that someone stop taking their medicine or go against doctor's orders. That is practicing medicine without a license and here in the US that will get you into trouble. If the person asks you about medication, tell them that they should ask God and get advice from their doctor. If the healing has started to manifest to the point they do not need medication, tests will confirm it.

In this chapter I want to give you a sample list of illnesses and common demonic roots. I am only including a few of the very common illness and their typical causes. I am totally convinced that a *rhema* word is needed for each person. I have really debated with myself about whether or not to give a list. The reason is that I have trained ministers to do healing by the *rhema* word and their results were extraordinary. Then I have seen them begin to rely on various lists that have been published, and their success rates have diminished. I warn you: **Please do not let this list be a replacement for the *rhema* word.** I just want you to begin to see the picture of how these things are linked. (I will shortly be telling you some more stories to show you how important it is to have a *rhema*).

ADD – attention deficit disorder. Double mindedness and self-rejection, also deaf and dumb spirit

Addictions – reduced serotonin levels. Low self-esteem and those things that accompany it.

Alcoholism – and other chemical additions – can be an allergy. Usually a generational familiar spirit.

Arthritis (inflammation of the joints) – bitterness and anger. Not being "jointly fit together" with the rest of the body.

Auto-Immune Diseases - the immune system mistakenly attacks itself, targeting the cells, tissues, and organs of a person's own body. Autoimmune diseases strike women more often than men; in particular, they affect women of working age and during their childbearing years. The spiritual implications are astonishing. As we attack ourselves spiritually, the body eventually agrees and starts attacking itself physically. This includes diseases such as MS, diabetes, lupus, psoriasis, etc. The roots of these diseases are often rejection, self-hatred, and guilt.

Back/Spine problems – spiritual alignment. Usually out of alignment with spiritual authorities. Doctors who deal with the back will tell you that a misalignment of the spine will cause inflammation or disease in various organs. We have heard of people receiving improved eyesight, restored hearing, even improved bladder control, when the issues of the spine were corrected. You may also need to deal with a demon of scoliosis, sciatica etc…

Cancer – cells in rebellion – caused by spirits of rebellion and regret. Curse it at the root. Look for rebellious behavior. Cast out spirit of cancer and rebellion or regret. Command both of the anti-oncogenes to be present and functional. [98]

Breast Cancer – conflict and resentment between females.
Liver Cancer – fornication, adultery, and/or pornography (Proverbs 7:21-23).
Hodgkins (cancer of Lymph) – bitterness and rejection from Father.
Leukemia (cancer of the Blood) – bitterness and rejection from Father.

Cholesterol – often found in people who are angry with themselves.

Endometriosis – can be caused by abortion – interruption in hormone cycle.

Fibromyalgia – often found in healthy females who tend to be stressed, tense, depressed, anxious, striving, driven, perfectionists. Deal with the spirit of fear and striving, also rejection and self hatred.

Gallstones – anger and resentment.

Headaches – witchcraft and/or guilt.

Manic Depression – inherited mental disease caused by a continual underproduction of serotonin as a result of a defect on the 27th lower right-hand side of the X chromosome.[99] Also spirit of depression.

Obsessive Compulsive Disorder – reduction in serotonin levels. Fear of man, fear of failure, fear of abandonment, fear of rejection, control spirit.

Osteoporosis – bone deterioration – envy and jealousy

results in rottenness of the bones (Proverbs 14:30)

Ovarian and Breast Cysts – relationship problems with mother or sister. Unresolved issues involving a breach, no fellowship.

Paranoid Schizophrenia – malfunction of two neurotransmitters – result in over-secretion of dopamine and serotonin. (see http://www.mentalwellness.com/html/mw/pd_schizophrenia.xml?article=schizophrenia.jspf) Two competing demons of rebellion and self-rejection.

Skin eruptions (rashes, humps, bumps, hives, and shingles) – anxiety, stress, and fear, usually coupled with self-rejection.

Vein problems – root is anger, rage and resentment – can be internalized.

Viruses – It is a life form that is capable of self action. It has an intelligence. Consider viruses to be "Spirits of Infirmity."

There are more comprehensive lists than this one. The purpose of this list is simply to give you a picture of the relationship that exists between body and soul. **I want to strongly emphasize again how necessary it is to have a word of knowledge, rather than a list, if you want to "heal them all."** Even though it is not always easy, the results are well worth the work.

You may have seen things on this list that we understand from medical science are a result of a chemical imbalance. For example, schizophrenia is the result of a chemical imbalance. How can a demon be at the root of this one? In the same way that extreme fear (which is usually as Spirit of Fear) can cause a rush of adrenaline, the demons behind schizophrenia can cause this chemical imbalance. Certain emotions can cause certain chemical reactions in your body.

I went to get my nails done one day and many of them were chipped or on the verge of breaking. I was beginning to develop a nail fungus on one of my fingers. The nail technician looked at my hands and declared, "You are stressed." I was amazed. It was true. My nail technician is not prophetic and I wondered how she knew this. Then she proceeded to tell me that she knew I was stressed because my immune system was so low that it did not fight off this fungus and that stress takes away what your nails and hair needs to be healthy.

During this same stressful time I was on a diet, trying to lose 15 pounds. I had tried all kinds of diets and even the most extreme ones were not working. I signed up with one of these doctor-supervised programs because I was not going to let 15 pounds get the best of me. I started on the program and all the girls running the clinic kept telling me how much I would lose, how great I would look. Week after week past and I lost nothing. Finally 3 weeks had past. I had lost nothing although I did everything they told me to do. I ate only what they told me. I exercised every day. I took all my supplements. Finally they declared that I was the only human being in the history of the company not to lose weight on this program and they had no answer. My answer came later while researching some medical terms for this book. Little did they know that I was under extreme stress during that time. The hormone cortisol is secreted by the adrenal glands in response to any kind of physical or psychological stress. Cortisol can stimulate weight gain and abdominal fat deposition.

Yes, your emotions can cause a chemical reaction in your body. Many times those emotions are under the control of demonic influences and that is the true root. This is why you must get to the root of the problem in order to get a person healed. This often requires a word of knowledge because not all things are evident on the surface.

Getting the word of knowledge regarding the root of the illness may take some effort, depending on how skilled you are and the state of your own emotions. If you think it is easy for me, let me tell you about Irene. She had advanced MS. This is an autoimmune disease. In this case, the immune system attacks the myelin sheath covering the muscles. The disease had progressed for many years. By the time I had the opportunity to minister to her, she was in a wheelchair and was severely crippled.

We prayed for a word of knowledge and I heard the Lord remind me that this was an autoimmune disease. I asked Irene if she had low self esteem or felt rejected in any way. To my surprise, she said, "No." I normally would not have believed it, but she said it in such a way that I felt like she was telling the truth.

I prayed more and heard the same words again: "This is an autoimmune disease." I questioned her in more detail. "Are you sure you never felt rejection from your husband, even after your body deteriorated? Are you sure that you never felt rejection from your family or friends or co-workers? Don't you have low-self esteem because of the condition of your body and your life?"

Each time the answer was "No."

I prayed harder and I heard the Lord say, "Mother." I zeroed in on this relationship. Irene again insisted that she and her mother had no problems. She said that her mother only had issues with her father. The two of them would verbally fight each other in such a vicious manner that she would often spend the night with her girlfriend to escape the war zone. I tried a different approach.

I asked, "Did you feel rejected when they fought? Did you ever think it was about you? Did you ever feel like you could have, or should have, fixed it?

All her answers were, "No." By then, I was feeling prophetically stupid.

Then the answer hit me like a lightening bolt! This was an autoimmune disease. That means one part of the body attacks another part of the body. Her parents were one flesh.[100] Spiritually speaking, one part of the flesh was attacking the other. **This "self attack" spirit had come down the generational line to Irene.**

We had her repent for receiving this spirit and broke her agreement with it. We commanded the spirit to leave and commanded the body to be healed. We were as specific as we could be in commanding the body. We commanded the immune system to stop attacking the myelin sheath. We commanded the sheath to be restored and the communication pathways to be reestablished.

Usually when we are praying for a believer, the healing will come by recovery, not by a miracle. Miracles are usually a sign for the unbeliever. We are promised the recovery, which is a process.[101] We are not promised the miracle, which is the instant result. Since I expected a recovery, I asked Irene what she wanted to see happen the most.

I do not like to send anyone home without getting breakthrough. The recovery process will take hours or days, but I know that I have broken through the blockage when something changes. The person receiving ministry may feel only 50% better, but that is acceptable for a beginning. I know that the recovery will continue once we have it started. We do not let our students stop praying until something changes.

Irene had not been able to feel her lower legs or feet for years. She wanted the feeling back. That became the target of our prayers. By the time we left that evening, Irene could feel her legs and feet and could move them on her own.

There were times that I wanted to quit that night (because I was embarrassed that I could not pin down the word of knowledge). How could I quit when she was still hanging in there? It took us more than two hours, but she agreed not to quit until we had the breakthrough. I believe it took two hours because I was not as good as Jesus was at hearing the Father's voice. The problem was not God, and it was not the sick person. It was my inability to hear God clearly and draw revelation from His words.

---

98 Wright, 138

99 Wright, 58

100 Genesis 2:24

101 Mark 16:18

Other, Not So Obvious, Causes of Sickness

I just want to mention a couple of other causes of illness that I think fall more in the curses category. The first one is involvement with the Free Masons. Ron Campbell has written an excellent book on the subject. What you will read next comes from his book, <u>Free from Freemasonary</u>.

A part of the secret rights of the Free Masons is to swear oaths and speak curses. Some of these curses are outright curses, and some are veiled ones. For example, one of the rituals every member must perform is to put on a blindfold and say, "I have long been in darkness and I now seek to be brought into the light."

These are unthinkable words for a believer to say! When people make the declaration, **with the breath of God**, that they are in darkness, **the power is there to bring that to pass.** An agreement is made that is not of God, and a door is created in the spirit realm.

There is also a ritual that involves putting a cable tow around the throat and chest and stomach. Then the man swears oaths such as, "If I ever divulge Masonic secrets I will have my throat cut from ear to ear, my heart torn out, be disemboweled, and my body cut in two." As a result, we find members of the Free Masons have a higher rate of throat disorders, heart and respiratory diseases and chronic stomach problems.

The families of Free Masons also have a higher rate of some plagues than the general population. These include:

➤ **Poverty** – perpetual financial insufficiency, fearful of not having enough, even with lots of money in the bank.

➤ **Barrenness and impotency**, together with miscarriages and female-related problems.

➤ **Divorce** – and other breakdown of family relationships

➤ **Chronic sickness** – heart problems, cancer, respiratory problems, allergies, throat ailments, strokes, attacks on the mind.

➤ **Defeat and failure** – unrealized potential

➤ **Mental illness**, torment and confusion

➤ **Traumas** – always putting out fires

➤ **Accident prone**

➤ **Premature and violent death**

When you are praying for healing and you suspect or you get a word relating to a curse from the Free Mason spirit, you should follow the procedure described earlier. Repent, renounce, and cast out.

Another unsuspected cause of illness due to a curse can

be found in 1 Corinthians 11:29-30. Paul is speaking here about what we have come to call communion. Jesus said, *"This is my body which is broken for you. This cup is the New Testament (covenant) in my blood."* This was the ancient language of covenant. Jesus was signaling the disciples that they were making covenant with Him. One of the required features of blood covenant was pronouncing of blessings and curses. It would not have been a legitimate covenant without it. Jesus declared, in verse 30, that the curse for breaking this covenant is sickness and death. These two things were almost always the curses for breaking blood covenant.

Concerning blood covenant, there is good news and bad news. Blood covenant was an all encompassing oath. When two people made blood covenant, they laid down their individual lives, and, with that, they laid down the right to refuse the other person any good thing. The penalty for breaking the blood covenant was sickness and death. We pledge to God, through the observance of the blood covenant called communion, that we lay down our individual lives. **When we make this pledge and then refuse God the good thing that He desires, we break covenant with Him**.

God does not take sickness and put it on us at that point. The sickness will come because we invite it with our actions. We open the door by our agreement with the enemy to not honor our commitment to God. That's the bad news.

To reverse the effects of this curse, follow the process mentioned earlier. Repent, renounce, and cancel that curse. I usually use words like this: "By the power of the Holy Spirit, I break the power of this curse. I command it to fall to the ground and bear no fruit." If you are interested in learning more about this, I hope to soon release a booklet on Blood Covenants.

The good news is that when we make covenant with Jesus, He makes covenant with us. He also lays down His individual life as well as His right to withhold any good thing from us. If we are walking in a covenant relationship with the Lord, we can ask for good things with much more confidence. He cannot deny us any good and perfect thing.

Section 5

How to Heal

The Healing Process

I had been praying for the ability to lay hands on the sick and see them recover for a long time. In my Christian circles, we all believed in healing, but you would never know it from our results. Some people we prayed for eventually recovered, usually with the help of medicine or a doctor. Most of them stayed the same, and some of them died. We felt completely out of control. So, my personal prayer was that I would be able to lay hands on sick people and see them **all** recover.

A few months after I renewed my prayer efforts in this direction, I heard the Lord say that I was to get trained in deliverance ministry. I could not believe the Lord said it to me! I had done some deliverance ministry and I hated it. It was messy and exhausting, and I did not want to deal with people's yucky stuff. I told a friend of mine what the Lord had said, and then I tried to forget about it.

A couple of months later, I heard the Lord clearly say that I was not just supposed to get training in deliverance, but I was supposed to become very skilled in this ministry. I nearly panicked! I was certain this meant that God was going to make me a deliverance minister, and the very thought of it made we want to quit ministry. I knew there was no way out, so I halfheartedly looked for a good deliverance ministry.

Several weeks later, my pastor's wife said that the Lord told her that if we would fast for 21 days, God would give us the key to healing. We all fasted for 21 days. There was no bolt of lightening, no revelation, no inspiration, just a brochure. The friend with whom I had shared the word God had given me about deliverance put a brochure in my hand announcing a deliverance conference. I cringed at the thought, but I did not know how to get out of it. I signed up for the conference, along with several other ladies. The conference was very useful and I learned several important things.

Shortly after our return, the deliverance minister at our church stepped down, and I was certain this must be the thing that God had in mind when He told me I had to learn deliverance. I volunteered to assist until we could find another person to fill that position.

Actually, I did not have to do as much deliverance as I imagined at church. That position was quickly filled. Also, with the revelation the Lord had given me about breaking agreement, it was no longer messy.

Word got out that I was doing this kind of ministry, and my phone started ringing. I had pastors from all denominations calling me, asking if they could come to me for personal deliverance. During this time I developed the expertise I needed to be really skilled at deliverance. To my surprise, I did not hate it as I thought I would. I ministered primarily in the area of deliverance for almost a year.

It was also about this time that I started taking prophetic training. That prophetic training (learning to recognize what the voice of God sounds like on the inside of me) was very useful in deliverance. I found I was able to get a *rhema* word of knowledge about what was operating in a person's soul.

The summer after I finished the prophetic training, I started to study healing. The big breakthrough in my revelation came when I put all the pieces together. **Jesus did healing by the *rhema* word each time,** and much of the time that He "healed" someone, He was casting out a demon. It finally dawned on me that God had been in the process of answering my prayers all along!

I had prayed to be able to lay hands on the sick and see them ALL recover. What I did not know at the time I prayed was that I needed a few extra skills to accomplish the task. If you want to heal the sick all the time, you need these two pieces of equipment – prophetic and deliverance. By prophetic, I mean that you have to be able to get a word from the Lord on the spot, and know what the voice of the Lord sounds like on the inside of you. The rest is easy.

Step By Step

By now, you have probably figured out the healing process. Here it is in all its simplicity:

1. Expect to be the one with the faith.
2. Get a *rhema* word. A Word of Knowledge about what has caused the sickness or what is blocking the healing.
3. Remove spiritual blockages through the deliverance process
   a. Repent
   b. Renounce
   c. Cast Out
4. Command the body
5. Thank the Lord

I will talk about each step. As you read on, please notice that only the last step is actually a prayer to the Lord. The rest is not praying, per se. You will **use the power of the**

Holy Spirit to impose the will of God on the earth. You are declaring, so get out of the mind set that you are just about to pray for healing. The idea that you should ask God for healing should be a dead issue by now. If it is not, go back and read sections 1-3 again.

We tell people **...if you will do everything we ask you to do, and you let us do everything we need to do, you will be healed**. If, by some chance you don't get healed right away, it is not God, it is not you; it is us – the ministers. Either we did not have faith, or we did not get the *rhema* word. We missed something. But we will stick with it as long as you will, and we will get you healed.

A friend of mine and I attended a conference. During this conference, the leader asked for people to come and pray for the sick. He singled us out and asked us to lay hands on this one particular lady. She was dying of some unknown cause. She had been a missionary and had to leave the mission field and come home. She had been to many doctors and they could not determine the cause. All her organs were disintegrating and no one knew why. She had received prayer for healing from her pastors and intercessors and she was not healed. She was in terrible pain.

We figured that there must be something blocking her healing if the prayer of faith did not work. So we prayed for a *rhema* word of knowledge. My friend and I both saw needles. One of us saw acupuncture needles and the other saw voodoo needles. She admitted she had been to a non-Christian acupuncturist. This was an open door for certain spirits to enter. She also admitted that she had been in a South American country ministering and was told that the local witch doctor had put a curse on her.

We prayed through all those issues and commanded the pain to leave, and her body to be healed. The pain immediately left for the first time. By the time we finished, we were the last ones to leave the room. We saw her the next day at the conference and she said that all her symptoms were gone. Praise God!

Then she said something that was almost unbelievable to me. We had spent a total of about 30 minutes getting her healed of a life threatening illness. She told us that no one had ever prayed that long for her before! I find it hard to believe that this woman, a missionary, had no one in her life who would pray for 30 minutes, or until they got a break-through! Don't quit until you see the results. This woman is alive today because someone spent 30 minute to hear from God for her. It took a *rhema* word for this case.

The One With The Faith

When I go to minister or teach healing, I expect NO ONE to have any faith. I expect to be the only one in the whole meeting with any faith. It is nice when someone brings their own faith, but I know that I cannot count on it. I have prayed for people with no faith and they have been healed. I have prayed for people that did not even believe in God, and they received miracles. If you don't have faith, go back to that section in the book and read on how to get faith.

Let me tell you where I started on my faith walk. I could not believe that I would get my answer, but I could believe that God is faithful. If I knew nothing else about God, I knew this: He is faithful. Even when I fail and I am not faithful, He is faithful. He may not be faithful to do what I want, but He is always faithful to His word. If I can find it in the word and I meet the conditions, then I can depend on Him to keep His word.

I know that God made His position on healing abso-lutely clear. Jesus suffered a painful death so that you could be free from sickness and disease. The Holy Spirit breathed instructions through the New Testament writers on what to do if we get sick. All the Godhead has participated in providing and confirming God's desire to heal us. When I have to summon my faith, I usually start there. God is faithful and He wants this person healed. The issue is never God's will to heal. He made His will perfectly known to those who want to know. He gave up his right to change His mind about it. He cannot make an exception in your case because His word is at stake. If you will do your part and not give up, the breakthrough will come.

Get The *Rhema*

I was reluctant to give you a list of diseases and causes. About half the time, a list like that will work. The rest of the time, you will not be successful unless you have a custom-tailored word for that individual. **We want to HEAL THEM ALL, so you must be able to get a *rhema* word.** Even when remembering the things on the list, I will not stop there.

We ministered to one woman who had cancer. She told us that all the women in her family died of breast cancer and she had just had her own breasts removed, even though they had no cancer, just because she was afraid of getting cancer. Knowing that she had this condition, I asked the Lord if it was a relationship problem with her mother or sister. Clearly I heard the word sister. So, I told her that this was rooted in the problem she had with her sister. She said that she had 5 of them.

So I asked the Lord, which one was it. I heard Him say the problem was rooted in the youngest one. When I told her this, she admitted it was the major issue of her life at that point. Her youngest sister just died. She was very angry with this sister because she had not told her that she was dying. She was also angry with all her other sisters because they had kept it a secret from her as well. The anger and bitterness caused the disease.

Other times I have had words of knowledge that you will never find on a list. I did a healing seminar out on the

West Coast. As is my custom, I asked if there was anyone there who was so sick that they were going to die if they did not get healed, and they had physical symptoms that we could observe. I selected a man named Bill. He had hepatitis E. There was no medication for this. His skin was red and he was wet with fever. His eyes were yellow. I asked all the students to gather around and get a word of knowledge. We all began to pray.

I got the word "motorcycle." I was panicked! I prayed, "Please God, this is my demo. Give me some word that makes sense."

I decided to stall. I asked all the students if they had a word. Several of them had words about addictions and drugs. All these words were true. We dealt with them, but Bill was still not healed. Finally, everyone was out of words and it was time for me to give mine. I took a deep breath and said, "I hear the word 'motorcycle.' What does that mean?" Everyone laughed because they knew Bill. I asked what was so funny.

Bill said, "They call me 'Motorcycle Bill' and I used to ride with Satan's Riders." Bingo!

The Lord had told him to get rid of the motorcycle, and it was still sitting in his garage. We had him repent, renounce, and then we cast out all the spirits associated with this cult. He was healed. His skin returned to normal color and his eyes changed color. I spoke to his pastor more than a year later and Bill was still healed. Praise God!

You will not find the word "motorcycle" on any list of roots of illnesses. You must understand that you cannot get healing 100% of the time **unless you will develop the ability to hear the voice of God on demand.**

Several years ago I was invited by an evangelist to go to Mexico on a mission trip to lead the prayer team. This was a last minute invitation and I only had three days to fast. At the end of those three days, the Lord told me that I would meet the "Spirit of Serpent" and I had authority over serpents. In the Bible, Satan is called the serpent. I assumed God was just telling me that I would encounter the work of Satan. I thought that was a strange way of telling me that I was going to come up against the enemy.

Once we arrived, we realized we had no one in charge of the deliverance room. If you have never ministered in a country where witchcraft is an everyday part of the culture, you can't imagine the demonic manifestations. As the gospel is being preached, the demons manifest and ushers have to drag people back to the deliverance room for ministry. The evangelist asked me to be in charge of this room. So, I thought for sure I would encounter the work of the enemy, the Serpent, there.

The last person I prayed for on the last night of the crusade was a 30 year old man. He was deaf and dumb and his little Mexican mother brought him to me. Without hesitating, I started commanding a deaf and dumb spirit to get out. No results. I spoke a little louder and firmer. No results. I then asked the mother if he was born this way. She said, "No, he saw something as a child that frightened him."

I said, "Ok, I've got it." Then I started commanding a spirit of fear to get out. No results. Then I asked the mother, "What did he see that frightened him?"

She said, "I was sitting under a tree, nursing him, and a snake fell out of the tree and landed on his head."

As soon as it registered with me, I jumped and shouted for joy! The mother thought I had lost my mind. I approached the man and very quietly whispered in his ear, "You Spirit of Serpent. I know your name. Get out!"

It did not appear that anything had happened, but I knew that something had to have changed. I looked at the man and whispered, "You can hear." He shook his head yes. I jumped up and shouted to him, "Say Jesus." He repeated it with little problem.

The man was instantly "healed." It looked like a miracle, but I think most miracle healings are really the result of removing the demonic so the body can function. And you will never find the words "Spirit of Serpent" on any healing list for deaf and dumb people.

Let me tell you one more incident. A man came to me with deafness in one ear. He had the problem for many years. I put my hand on his ear and prayed for a word. I heard the Holy Spirit say the words "mind control." I asked the man about this and he admitted that he was involved in a form of witchcraft, and the goal of all witchcraft is to control the mind and will of others. I had him repent and renounce this. I cast out the spirit of mind control and everything attached to it. His ear popped open and he could hear. Again, this looked like a miracle, but really it was removing the demon that blocked his healing. You will not find the words "mind control" on any healing list for deaf people.

I hope I have made my point. It is fine to look at the list and cover the common causes, but unless the healing manifests, do not stop at the list. Jesus had a *rhema* word every time. If we want the same results, we need the same methods.

Remove The Blockage

Remember the premise of getting a word of knowledge; the reason for the *rhema*. If the person is a believer, then that person has the right to be healed. If he or she has followed scripture and called for the elders, and if the elders really had faith when they prayed, and they commanded the healing instead of asking God to heal, this person should be healed. If this believer has received the proper ministry and is not healed, then there is something blocking the healing. It is up to you to remove that blockage. Once the blockage is removed, the body will most likely heal itself. But, I am getting ahead of myself.

To remove the blockage, simply deal with the curse or

demonic activity that is operating. Whenever I am ministering this part, I use certain words. It is not like they are some sort of magic formula, but it establishes the basis for the ministry. I tend to begin with these words, "**In the name of Jesus and by the power of the Holy Spirit...**" This reminds me, and tells any spirit of darkness, that it is not my power or righteousness that is the issue. It is the righteousness of Jesus and the power of the Holy Spirit that are in operation. If it is a curse, I break the curse. I usually use words like this:

> "In the name of Jesus and by the power of the Holy Spirit, I break the curse of poverty that has been on Cheryl. I command this curse to fall to the ground and bear no fruit. I command all spirits associated with this curse to get out of Cheryl's life. I break the recompense of any words or actions that have brought this curse or other works of the enemy. I remit the sins and declare that they can never be held to Cheryl's account again. I hereby forbid the enemy from extracting a penalty from Cheryl based on prior bad acts. I bless her with the blessings of Jehovah and declare than none can curse whom God has blessed."

Sometimes you will find demonic spirits in layers. You will get a *rhema* word and you know that you have heard from God. But when you cast out that spirit, nothing happens. Don't stop.

For example, maybe the person has been involved with witchcraft and now has headaches. Casting out the spirit of witchcraft will usually work, but you may also have to cast out a spirit of control and manipulation. Those involved in witchcraft are often either the victims of control and manipulation or they use control and manipulation on others. You may not see the results until you cast out everything that is attached to witchcraft.

When doing healing, we generally do not stop ministering until the person tells us something has changed. We then assume that we have gotten rid of the blockage and the body is beginning to recover. The person does not have to be totally recovered before we stop. I believe my goal is to get the healing started by removing the blockage.

If there is no change in the person's physical symptoms, you (the minister) have missed something. There are no excuses. It isn't that the person has some hidden sin in his or her life. It is your job to identify that sin and deal with it. It isn't that God has a special timing for the person's healing. Sickness is a demonic work, and God does not want people to live under demonic oppression even one minute, much less days or weeks. The sickness is not a way for God to teach the person something. See sections 1-3. If that person is not healed, having willingly come to you for healing, it means that you, as the minister, have missed something.

There are times when people don't really want to be healed because they get attention or some secondary gain from the illness. Then...good luck trying to get them healed. I have learned to deal with this up front. I will hardly ever pray for someone who is only there because someone else made him come. But, if a person comes to me and really wants to be healed, then the only reason the person is not healed is my failure in some area, usually word of knowledge. Part of the task of becoming a healing minister is to accept responsibility for your failures. I have ministered to some people more than once to get them healed because I missed something the first time.

Command The Body

Let me remind you. You are not yet at the praying-to-God part. You are still using the authority delegated to you by

Jesus and the power of the Holy Spirit. Mark 11:23 says, *"If you say to this mountain, be removed..."* **Jesus did not tell you to ask God to do it, but, rather, He told you to speak to the mountain.** When Jesus did healing, He did not ask God to do anything. He spoke what should happen and it did.

Don't say, "Well, that was Jesus." I will remind you that everything Jesus did, He did by the power of the Holy Spirit[102] This was not a different version of the Holy Spirit, but the same one that you have.

You speak to sickness and you command the body. If the blockage has been removed, the body has to obey. Most bodies will recover on their own once the blockage is removed.

I recently heard of a famous Buddhist monk who is amazing his followers by doing healing. He diagnoses the things in the soul which are causing conditions in the body. If bitterness is the cause for their arthritis, then he tells them to get bitterness out of their souls. When the people deal with the issues of their souls, their bodies begin to heal. Of course, since he does not have the ability to get a word of knowledge from God, he cannot heal them all. But, he can work off a list the same as you.

Why then do we command the body, if it will pretty much heal itself over time? There are a couple of reasons. We have found that the more we command the body, using the power of the Holy Spirit, the faster the recovery will come. Also, the more specific we are with our commands, the faster the recovery. Since we do not want to stop praying until we know we have removed the blockage, we need to do this part to see if we can see a change before we stop ministering. We generally do all these steps, including the thanking-God part, which I will discuss next, before we stop to assess the situation. If nothing has changed, then we start over.

When commanding the body, speak with authority and

tell it what you want it to do. I generally say something like this:

> "I speak to Cheryl's body, and by the power of the Holy Spirit I command it to be healed. Immune system, I command you to recognize this virus as the enemy and to quickly manufacture antibodies for this virus. I command the cells in the body to purge any virus. I command the receptors for this virus to reject this virus, rather than link with it. I forbid this virus to reproduce in this body. I command this body to eliminate all remnants of this virus quickly."

I said it earlier, and I will say it again. If you don't know much about a disease, ask the person who is sick how it works. Believe me, if they have had it for any length of time, they have been on the internet and spoken with doctors and friends, and they can tell you all about it. Then sometimes you will get a word of knowledge about what to command.

Remember the story about the doctor who had anxiety attacks? The Lord told me to command his serotonin levels. I did not even know the function of serotonin, and I did not know if he had too much or not enough. So, I commanded it to be adequate and at the proper level.

When commanding healing, I almost always start with pain. If the person is in pain, get rid of it first. Pain is the easiest thing to heal. Pain is a symptom, not a root. You can command pain to go before you even get to the roots of the problem. But remember, the pain will come back if the roots are not addressed.

I was doing a healing clinic in a city in Mexico. For my demo, I asked if there was anyone there with pain. A young man raised his hand and said that he had pain in his knees. I called him up front and began to command the spirit of pain to leave and all inflammation and swelling to go. I commanded his nerve endings to stop manifesting pain. In just a few minutes, the young man was pain free.

The young man's doctor was in the audience and he came and scolded me. He asked me why I had done that. The young man was severally overweight and the pain in his knees was a result of his weight. The doctor had been trying to get him to lose weight and he would not. Now he was afraid that this young man would never lose weight. "Don't fear," I told the doctor. "The pain will return unless he deals with the root."

"If the pain will come back, why deal with it?" you might ask.

There are a couple of reasons. First, it makes the person more comfortable receiving ministry. Sometimes it might take two hours to get someone healed if they have lots of issues. You don't want them in pain for those two hours; you want them comfortable and able to concentrate on what you are saying or asking. The second reason is that it raises your faith and theirs. If they begin to believe that this might work, then they are more open and cooperative.

Sometimes, pain will not go with a simple command. In this case, the pain is connected to a pain in the soul. In order to get rid of the pain in the body, you must get rid of the pain in the soul. When you remove the soul pain, you may not even have to kick out the body pain; it most likely will leave on its own.

---

[102] Acts 10:38

Thanksgiving

I learned the importance of thanksgiving from Pastor Buddy Malloy. He opened my eyes to see what was hidden in plain view in the scriptures. I have incorporated it into everything I do and teach. It has changed my life and the lives of countless others. With his permission, I will share some of those treasures with you now.

You are never finished with a healing session until you have given thanks. In fact, I have had great miracles happen while giving thanks. The Bible tells us that there is a specific, unique power in thanksgiving. I will keep referring to this scripture, and by the time you are done with this chapter, you'll have that scripture memorized. It's 1 Thessalonians 5:18:

> *"In everything give thanks, for this is the will of God in Christ Jesus concerning you."*

"In" everything give thanks. Notice it doesn't say "for" everything. Not everything is from God. So, you're not going to thank God for your sickness, which came from the enemy. But in spite of it, in the midst of it, you are to thank God.

You may be thinking of Ephesians 5:20:

"Giving thanks always for all things unto God and the Father in the name of our Lord Jesus Christ;

The word "for" in this verse is the Greek word *huper*. It is best (and usually) translated "above, beyond, or over." You can see an example of this same word translated as the word "over" just a couple of chapters earlier in this same letter to the church at Ephesus. Ephesians 3:20 *"And hath put all things under his feet, and gave him to be the head over all things to the church,"* By using one of these words such as "over," Ephesians 5:20 becomes consistent with 1 Thessalonians – in, above, or over all things, give thanks! Since using this word brings more harmony within the Scriptures, it should be considered a better choice.

I know that it bothers some people when we reinterpret the words that they have come to count on for so many years. It almost feels heretical to change the translation of a word. I confronted the same issue when I went to seminary and learned that I had misunderstood many things because of poor English translations. I felt like we could not change anything because the Word of God is sacred and divinely inspired.

This is what helped me and I offer it to you. What we really believe is that the ORIGINAL is sacred and divinely inspired. The translations were all done by men who had their own interpretive bias. When given a choice of words to use, they chose the one that best fit their understanding of God's intention. It may or may not have been the best choice. Also, there was never just one person who translated the whole Bible. It was a team of people and each one brought their own thoughts to the effort. I have come to learn that if two verses seem to be in conflict with one another, one of them was translated wrong.

Back to thanks…

David said, *"You prepare a table before me in the midst of my enemies."* [103] **In the middle of the problem is where you want to give thanks**. It will cause the situation to turn around. So in spite of the problem, you should give thanks.

Psalms 92:1 says, *"It is a good thing to give thanks unto the Lord and sing praises to His name."* And this word "good" in the Hebrew means "beneficial." God is saying, "Let Me show you a treasure here. It's beneficial to you to give thanks."

I believe priests and prophets of The Old Testament had a revelation concerning thanksgiving. In 1 Chronicles 16:1-4 we read the story of David bringing the ark into Jerusalem. They were getting ready to have a praise service. Actually, it was really like a thanksgiving service. In this story, David made specific appointments. He appointed certain Levites to minister before the ark of the Lord, and to record, and to thank, and to praise the Lord God of Israel. David knew that it was important to not only take territory, but to protect territory.

I believe that David had the revelation that praise defeats the enemy and thanksgiving protects what you have. David wrote a song for this occasion to thank the Lord. You see it in verse eight. It says,

"Give thanks unto the Lord, call upon His name,
make known His deeds among the people."

That was David's idea of how to protect yourself, and how to do spiritual warfare. Apparently he thought it was so important that he subsidized people to do it full time. In 1 Chronicles 23:30, it says he appointed Levites to thank and praise twice a day. Those two elements – praise being the offensive weapon, thanksgiving being the defensive weapon – may have very well been David's secret of success.

King Hezekiah saw a revival in the nation when he became king. You can read about it in 2 Chronicles 31:2. One of the first things that Hezekiah did when he got to be king was to reinstitute the particular activity of thanking and praising God twice a day. When he did that, the nation of Israel experienced revival.

We can find another powerful mention of thanksgiving in the story of Daniel. Daniel's usual custom was to pray three times a day. The other princes of the kingdom were jealous and conspired against Daniel. They persuaded the king to make a new law forbidding requests to anyone, except the king. They did this, knowing that Daniel would pray to God. What did Daniel do when the decree was signed? He prayed and gave thanks, as was his usual custom, even though he knew that his actions were a death sentence against him. What would you do?

> *"Now when Daniel knew that the writing was signed, he went in to his house, and his windows being opened in his chamber towards Jerusalem, he kneeled upon his knees three times a day and he prayed and he gave thanks before his God as he did all the time."* [104]

Daniel was in an untenable situation. There was no way to win. He could not displease God to save his own life. Daniel's solution – give thanks. You know the rest of the story. The mouths of the lions were shut. Huge miracle! Remember, **when you are thanking God, the lions cannot chew on you.**

Paul picked up on this revelation. In Colossians 4:2 Paul gives this advice:

> *"Continue in prayer and watch in the same with thanksgiving."*

The word "watch" means "to be vigilant, to rise, to stay awake, to give strict attention to, to be cautious." It means to take heed lest, through laziness, some destructive calamity overtake you.

Some things you can get in prayer, but if you don't watch over them with thanksgiving, you're going to lose them. You're going to get robbed of the thing with which God just blessed you. Some people get robbed of their blessing before they even get to enjoy it. They're really good at using their faith to get it, but then they can't hang onto it, and they don't know why. **Thanksgiving is a form of watching over what you have.**

Paul gives us great insight into this mystery in 1 Corinthians 10:10. Here he is speaking of the Israelites in the wilderness. It says here, *"Neither murmur, as some of them also murmured, and were destroyed by the destroyer."*

Paul was saying that, if you murmur and complain, you are inviting the destroyer to come and steal all your stuff and destroy you. It seems we need to do two things. First, don't mummer and complain. Second, give thanks in all things. Remember the story of the coyote? **Whining and complaining actually attracts the demonic.**

John wrote in John 10:10 about the destroyer. *"The devil comes to steal, to kill, and to destroy."* Thanksgiving is the way to guard against the destroyer. The opposite of thanksgiving is murmuring and complaining.

As you pray for people who need healing, you will run across those who have had their health destroyed by the destroyer. The root cause is murmuring and complaining. I have a good friend who is in healing ministry with me. She has gotten herself healed of all kinds of things. The one thing from which she was having trouble getting healed was an outbreak on her arms. She had gone to the doctor and he knew no cure for it.

Then one day she had the insight she needed. For almost

all of her life she had hated the way her arms looked. They were heavier than she liked, and she murmured and complained about them, bringing a curse to them. Sure enough, that is where the enemy had his deepest stronghold!

Think about it. I am not talking about throwing a casual "Thank You" God's way every once in a while. For David it was an institution. For Daniel, it was a lifestyle. Notice that the Word says Daniel prayed and gave thanks "as he did every day." An effective "watch" of thanksgiving means living a lifestyle of thankfulness. It is being thankful all the time. I wake up in the morning and almost the first words out of my mouth every morning are, "Thank you, God. I love the life that you've given me. I appreciate you. I thank you for the truth that you've shown me, for where you lead me." I constantly thank Him.

I like the way Pastor Buddy says it: "Most of us are either thinking or we're thanking." Actually, thanking is a way to get hold of your thinking. Ephesians 5:4 says,

> *"Let no one be able to accuse you of any of these kinds of thing. Dirty stories, foul talks, coarse jokes, they are for not for you. Instead, remind each other of God's goodness and be thankful."*

One way to start controlling your thought life is to speak of God's goodness and be thankful. If you have an issue of fear, the way to overcome it is to speak of God's goodness and be thankful.

Did you know that **you cannot remove a thought; you can only replace a thought?** Let me prove it to you. Don't think of orange. Don't think of how it looks. Don't think of the fruit orange. Don't think of how it is round, when you peel it that certain citric smell seems to burst forth. Don't think of it.

How did you do? It's impossible to not think of it, unless

you think of something else – replace the thought. So, when the spirit of fear comes, what are you going to do? You have to replace the thought of fear with a thought of God's goodness and thankfulness. Think of Psalms 139: *He is before me, He is behind me... He has completely surrounded me... His hand is always on me...He knows my words before I've even spoken them... He knows my thoughts when they are far off. Where can I go from his presence?* Replace the thought and give thanks.

Let's look at it again. Paul said not to let anyone accuse you of these things. Then he talked about a whole bunch of negative things. He said that, instead of doing these things, we are to remind each other of God's goodness. Do you remember when Israel would get together before a battle, and recount the goodness of the Lord? They would say, "The God who brought us out of Egypt, who brought us to the Red Sea, who parted the Red Sea, who kept us in the wilderness, who gave us the law, etc..." **That was their way of replacing any thoughts of fear and defeat before a battle.**

My favorite story of thanksgiving is found in Nehemiah, chapter twelve. The book of Nehemiah starts with Nehemiah lamenting the broken-down walls of Jerusalem. Nehemiah led a group of people back to Jerusalem, and they rebuilt the walls around the city. Chapter 12 tells of the dedication of the walls. I will skip through this chapter because I only want to make one point.

In verse 8 we find that Nehemiah appointed supervisors of thanksgiving. In verse 9 we see he appointed two foremen for the supervisors of the watch of thanksgiving. So they actually had a watch of thanksgiving going on. These troupes stood on opposite sides of the wall in what Nehemiah calls "watches." It is very insightful of him to identify it in this unusual way, as guard duty "watches of thanksgiving," because that was exactly what was happening.

Nehemiah was undoubtedly familiar with some of the writings of the Old Testament. David lived at least 600 years before Nehemiah. Maybe Nehemiah saw what happened when David gave thanks and the nation was protected. Maybe he read about the revival under Hezekiah, when a nation experienced rebirth. Maybe he got his revelation directly from God. The point is that Nehemiah used a formula for the protection of God that was tried and proven. He appointed people to give thanks.

Then we read more about these troupes in verses 31, 38, and 40. In verse 31, he tells how he brought the princes of Judah up on the wall. Don't miss the fact that Nehemiah points out these men were from the tribe of Judah. They were known as the wild praisers. He then divided them into *"two great companies of them that gave thanks."* One went on the right hand wall. In verse 38 he tells us, *"...the other company of them that gave thanks went over against them."* Then, we read in verse 40 that the two great companies were in place, along with Nehemiah and half of the rulers with him. Verse 42 says that the singers sang loud.

So here is the picture. Nehemiah did not take beggars off the street or the poor, unskilled, and unemployed to do this job. He took the princes of Judah. He sent half of them around one side of the wall while he took the other half and placed them on the other half of the wall. When they were in position, they were standing on the wall facing each other. They sang loudly the "Thanks of The Lord." By doing this, they created a canopy of thanksgiving over their city. **This canopy of thanksgiving was a defensive weapon; it was a protective weapon.** This was Nehemiah's idea of a "watch."

This should become our idea of a watch too! Remember the definition of the word "watch?" Be sober, be vigilant, watch. How do you do that? Thanksgiving. Jeshua and Zerubbabel did not forget to give thanks when they rebuilt the altar. You can read about it in Ezra 3:11.

Jesus was another person who had a revelation of the power of thanksgiving. What did Jesus do when He needed a miracle? His disciples had come to accept His healing people and casting out demons as something easy and common-place, but when it came to feeding five thousand people, even his disciples were unbelievers. This miracle of feeding so many with so little was another story. **It took an entirely different set of skills**. Think of it. All you have is some-one's sack lunch. Probably by this time the disciples had figured out that healing was not such a hard thing. Get a *rhema*, if you need to, kick out a demon, command the body. Piece of cake! But feed five thousand with a boy's lunch?

I love the way the gospel writer John wrote because he told things other writers didn't tell. He was very intent on proving Jesus' Messiahship so you pick up a lot of details from John that the other gospel writers left out.

John chapter 6 tells us about the feeding of the five thou-sand. In verse 11 we find the secret of this miracle: "*And Jesus took the loaves, and when He had given thanks, He distributed to the disciples.*"

John included the words, "*and when He had given thanks.*" He didn't want you to miss it. That was an impor-tant part of the feeding five-thousand. As a matter of fact, it was so important that he repeated it when he was telling the story the following day, beginning in verse 22. In verse 23 we read, "*…near the place where they did eat bread, after that the Lord had given thanks.*" So, he's telling the story the next day about what had happened the previous day. He not only mentioned it in the first account, but just a few verses later he reminds them that the giving of thanks was a vital part of the whole thing. John did not want the reader to miss the connection between the giving of thanks and feeding five-thousand.

This is not the only time we see Jesus in need of a huge miracle. He had healed others and had even raised the dead, but as he stood in front of the tomb of Lazarus, He needed something extra. You see, Lazarus was what was known as a "fourth-day man."

Rabbis believed that any decent prophet could raise someone from the dead if that person had been dead three days or less. After all, both Elijah and Elisha had done so. However, no one had ever raised someone from the dead that had been dead for four days. The rabbis believed the soul hung around the body for three days, hoping a prophet would come and raise the body. But they believed that, after the fourth day, the soul departed and resurrection was not possible. Jesus stood at the tomb of a "fourth-day-man." This would probably be considered the most spectacular miracle of His life.

What did Jesus do when He needed a huge miracle? He turned His face toward Heaven, and the first words out of His mouth were... you guessed it... *"Thank You, Father."* [105] He found something to be thankful for in that very moment. Jesus needed a huge miracle, and the way He knew to get a huge miracle was to enter into the presence of His Father with the words, "Thank you." He thanked God that He always heard Him and that they always had that intimate, constant communication. It makes me think of 1 John 5:15:

> *"And if we know that He hears us, whatsoever we ask, we know that we have the petitions that we desired of Him."*

Jesus expressed thankfulness for the only thing that was the issue. Jesus thanked His Father that He heard Him. Because, if He hears us, we have what we desire. This was the "prayer of faith" for Jesus. He had faith in the word of God. Although this verse had not yet been penned, Jesus knew all things from the Father, Who taught him. Jesus was the Word personified. Jesus put His faith in the promise of

His Father and expressed His thanks for the promise that He knew would bring the results. Jesus rested His faith on the promise. Do you remember what I said about the prayer of faith? **If you really believe that you have what is promised, what is there left to do but give thanks?**

Jonah, in the belly of the whale, decided to put this principle to work in his life. I almost couldn't believe it when I saw this. We read in Jonah 2:1 that "*Jonah prayed, unto the Lord his God out of the fish's belly.*" Of course he prayed. Wouldn't you?

Then in verse 9 we find out what he prayed: "*I will sacrifice unto You with the voice of thanksgiving.*" Do you think maybe Jonah had the revelation that he, since he had murmured and complained, was now in the belly of a whale? "Okay, if my murmuring and complaining got me here, I know what's going to happen next. I will be destroyed by the destroyer."

God had told Jonah to go prophesy to the inhabitants of the city of Nineveh. Jonah had refused. He had complained to God that he would go and prophecy destruction and the people would repent and God would spare them. He would look like a fool. It was whining and complaining, and it got him a bit of time in the belly of the whale. But in that situation he knew what to do. "*I will sacrifice to You with the voice of thanksgiving.*" What happened next? The fish vomited Jonah out. Does it remind you of Daniel and the lions' den? It reminds me of it. The only thing these two stories have in common is thanksgiving. If you are a Jonah, remember that the one who devoured you cannot hold you when you are thanking.

Back to 1 Thessalonians 5:18:

"*In all things give thanks, for this is the will of God concerning you.*"

If you are not giving thanks, you are actually out of the will of God! Did you catch that? So many people say, "I just wish I knew what the will of God was for my life." I can tell you what His will is; *"In all things give thanks, for this is the will of God in Christ Jesus concerning you."*

If you are trying to reach your destiny, if you are trying to move forward, if you are trying to become that person in the vision God gave you, but you are whining and complaining, you are flat <u>out</u> of the will of God. You are on the wrong path. Remember, **you are not thanking Him for everything; you are thanking in spite of everything.** So, let us say that you just lost your job. What are you going to do? You are going to thank Him in the midst of that situation.

> "Thank You, God, that You, and not that company, are my source. I thank You, God, that before I was ever formed in my mother's womb You knew this day I would call on You and You already had a plan. I thank You for Your foresight; I thank You for Your care of me; I thank You that You have gone before me and prepared the way. Father, I rest in Your abundant provision. I celebrate what You are about to do, even though I haven't seen it. I know it is going to be so good because You are so good to me."

Give Him wild exuberant praise and thank Him. If you do this, you will spend less time in the problem.

The word "thanks" in the original Greek is the word Eucharist or *eucharistos*. It means "good favor" or "to be well favored." It contains the word *charis,* which means "grace." So, **every time you thank God in that situation, you are imparting grace to that situation.**

For years we have said "grace" over our food. But somewhere along the way we lost the understanding that, when we thank God for something, we've just added grace to it. Think of it as a baking ingredient. Into each situation you add some grace by thanking God in the midst of that situation.

Never make a permanent decision based on a temporary condition. Never make a permanent decision until you've added grace to the situation and see what the grace of God does to that situation.

It is kind of hard to know the will of God when you are not operating in the will of God. If you are unthankful then you are out of the will of God, and Romans 1:21 will scare you.

"Because when they knew God, they glorified him not as God, neither were they thankful."

They did not recognize God in their situation, and they were not thankful. Watch what happens to a people who do not praise God and do not give thanks to Him. The second half of that verse says,

"They became vain in their imaginations and their foolish hearts were darkened."

I have people who come to me that say, "I feel like I'm in the dark; I can't figure out what I'm supposed to be doing, and I can't see the light at the end of the tunnel. It's like I'm in this dark place."

I know exactly what the diagnosis is. How do you get in a dark place? Don't praise God, don't give Him thanks. Then your foolish heart will become darkened and you won't be able to see the will of God anymore. It gets worse. Look at verses 22-25.

"Professing themselves to be wise, they became fools and changed the glory of the incorruptible God into an image like to corruptible man and birds and

four footed beasts and creeping things. Wherefore God also gave them up to uncleanness through the lusts of their own hearts, to dishonor their own bodies between themselves: Who changed the truth of God into a lie and worshiped and served the creature more than the creator, who is blessed be forever, amen"

Let me just say something about the last part of this verse. Do you know how you worship the creation more than the creator? You say things like, "I was made this way. I cannot change. This is who I am." When you say these things, you are saying that the creature is supreme. "I was born this way. I'll always be this way. Nothing can change it." Then you have just elevated the creature higher than the creator. When you are stubborn and you've got your own opinion and it won't be changed, you are worshiping the creature more than the creator. Now, here is the really scary part. Look at verse 26:

"For this cause God gave then up to vile affections: for even their women exchanged their natural use to that which was against nature: And likewise also the men, leaving the natural use of the women, burned in their lust one towards another, men with men working that which is unseemly and receiving in themselves the recompence of their error which was meet."

So, this tells us that the pathway to homosexuality starts with not giving praise to God, being unthankful, and worshiping the creature more than the creator. Actually, if you think about it, the beginning of homosexuality is unthankfulness. "I'm not thankful for the way God made me. I should have been in a different body. I got trapped in the wrong thing. I should have been a man (or I should have been a woman) and I'm unthankful, and I don't like this about me."

I see the most beautiful young people, teenagers, twenty year olds, pick themselves apart. "You know, my hair is just, you know, it's ugly, and I've got this little mole right here, and look at this little wart on my skin! Isn't it terrible?" They are not perfect, and they murmur and complain and they are unthankful.

If you want to open the door for the enemy to destroy your life, say the following things: "I don't like my life. My legs are too skinny, I'm too tall, I'm too fat, I'm too short, I'm too something. And I'm unthankful for the person that You created me to be, God." Satan will be on your doorstep in short order to say, "Oh well, let me make you a different person. Try this. Try this. Try this."

If you find people who are in the trap of homosexuality and you're doing deliverance, **one of the issues that you must address is their unthankfulness about the person God created them to be.** I am <u>not</u> suggesting that they be thankful that they're trapped in homosexuality.

People who are involved in homosexuality will tell you that it is in the genes. "How are you going to fight your own genes? God made me this way. I was born this way. How can it be a sin if I was born this way and I have no control over it?"

So, which verse do you pull out? How about John chapter 9? The man was born blind, but he didn't stay blind after Jesus touched him. **So the condition of his birth was not the perfect will of God.** The condition of his birth carried the mark of the enemy. How do we know this? Because Jesus came to destroy the works of the enemy. [106]

Take a look at what Jesus destroyed, and you will recognize the work of the enemy. Did he destroy the blindness that was on the man from birth? Yes. So, there was a work of the enemy on someone from birth. It didn't stay on him after Jesus touched him.

You are not going to win an argument by debating whether people were or were not born that way, or is there a gene. Don't debate it. Go ahead and give them this answer: "Okay, let's say there is a gene; let's say you were born this way. It doesn't matter. You don't have to stay that way. When Jesus touches you, it will change. So now, don't tell me you have no choice. Do you want Jesus to touch you and take it away?" It's just a demon. It came in through unthankfulness and rejection.

So, the final stage of unthankfulness is destruction and abandonment of who you were made to be. I know that I mentioned this earlier, but now is a good time to remember it. In 2 Corinthians 10:4-5, we are told that strongholds are thoughts and imaginations. That is why, in deliverance, our target is the agreement. The demon will let go when the agreement is destroyed.

The next issue to address is idolatry. One definition of idolatry is worshiping your own opinion. King Saul is an example. We read in 1 Samuel 15:23 that Samuel told Saul, *"Rebellion is as the sin of witchcraft and stubbornness is as iniquity and idolatry."* When you are stubborn, and you have your own opinion, and no one can change it, you are worshiping your own opinion. You've made it supreme. Stubbornness is idolatry. So the next step is wicked and immoral imagination, which results in uncleanliness and homosexuality. It all begins with not giving God glory and being unthankful. Isn't that scary?

Review

Why did I teach about thanksgiving in this book on healing? Because thanksgiving is part of our process for getting somebody healed. Let's review the process. If people are believers, and if they have already received prayer for healing, and they are not healed, something is blocking the healing. You should get a word of knowledge to find out what is blocking the healing.

Next, evict whatever demonic spirit you find. Command the body to be healed. You are NOT asking God to heal. You're ordering the body to obey your words. The more specific you can be, the quicker you will see the results. So, if the sickness is the heart, you say, "Heart I command you to be healed." But if you know they have a mitral valve prolapse, then speak right to the mitral valve. Say, "Mitral valve, I command you to be healed and not to leak at all and to function, and I command that the tissue of the mitral valve become strong and be restored."

You are not finished with the healing until you thank God for the healing. This is the prayer of faith. This is Jesus standing at the tomb of Lazarus. This is the prayer over the fishes and loaves. The job is not complete until you have done this part.

I'm not asking you to do the old faith thing and just confess, confess, confess. I am asking you to thank Him for what you know is already true, not what you hope might be true.

"Thank You, God, that Your healing power IS WORKING in my body to bring a full recovery. Thank You, God, that You are faithful to Your word. Thank You that You have set me free from the plans the enemy had to destroy me. Thank You, God, that You are my great physician. Thank You, Jesus, that you did not just die that I could live eternally, but You were wounded that I could be healed in this lifetime. Thank You, Lord, for sharing with me the power of the Holy Spirit; not a different Holy Spirit, but the same Holy Spirit that was in Jesus."

I think you get the idea.

Let me share one last story. We have seen many people healed while we are doing the thanking rather than when we cast out a spirit or command the healing. Usually when I teach a healing seminar, the last day of the seminar is for the students to invite their families and friends to be healed. The students practice what they have learned on these people. I was in another country teaching one such healing clinic. It was Saturday and the clinic was packed with people waiting to be healed. A young man came into the clinic and waited for quite some time to be healed. Finally, he asked me if I would just pray for him so he could leave. He was in his twenties and looked quite healthy to me. As I found out, Alex was an athlete and he had injured his knee playing sports. He just needed it healed.

I quickly sat him down and began to pray to see if there was anything demonic blocking the healing. He was a nice Christian man and others had prayed for his healing. I did not hear anything that would be an issue with his knee. So I commanded the knee to be restored and began thanking God for the healing.

There was an unusual anointing on that thanking prayer. I wept and wept about how good God was to us to have provided healing for us before we even needed it. I prayed something like this:

> "Thank you God that you made us your children. Thank you that you gave us your Holy Spirit so that we have power over sickness just as Jesus did. Thank you that you did not give us a different version of the Holy Spirit, but the same version Jesus had; the same Holy spirit that....."

What came out of my mouth next shocked me. I get the same surprised reactions from others with whom I have shared this story. Although everyone admits what I am about to say next is obvious, no one had every thought of it before. I finished that sentence:

> "...the same Holy spirit that hovered over the torn and mangled body of Jesus and healed it."

As I spoke these words I saw a vision of the Holy Spirit hovering or brooding over the dead and torn body of Jesus and recreate it, restore it. This was much of the same picture I imagine when I read the words in Genesis 1:2 where the Holy Spirit brooded of the waters at creation.

I had never considered this before. Of course we never think of Jesus being sick and so naturally we do not think of Jesus needing healing. But He did. His flesh was torn from His body and His muscles were torn. Yet, when He appeared to the disciples, He told Thomas, touch My hands and My side.[107] Jesus had scars of the abuse. Those scars were the proof to Thomas. Jesus had been healed and He had the scars to prove that the flesh had healed. Romans 8:11 says:

> *"But if the Spirit of him that raised up Jesus from the dead dwell in you, he that raised up Christ from the dead shall also quicken your mortal bodies by his Spirit that dwells in you."*

We all know from this verse that the Holy Spirit raised Jesus from the dead, but the truth is that the Holy Spirit also healed Him. This word raised is the Greek word *egeiro*. The meaning includes: to wake or rouse from sleep, disease, or death. That is the power that is walking around inside of you.

As I got this revelation, and spoke it out, Alex declared that the pain in his knee was gone. I insisted that he get up and jump on the knee or twist it or something. He was cautious, but he tried it. The knee was totally and completely healed by a miracle restoration.

I found out his story later. Alex was a professional athlete. He played on a national football team and was the national athlete of the year the previous year. He was a strong Christian witness in the professional sports field. Training camp was set to start in two weeks and his career was ended if he did not get a miracle.

Praise God! Alex was totally healed that day. I spoke with his pastor almost a year later and asked about him. He told me that Alex had played all season with no injury and his team had won the championship again.

Don't forget the thanking part!

---

[103] Psalms 23:5

[104] Daniel 6:10

[105] John 11:41

[106] 1 John 3:8

[107] John 20

More Training

I hope you have enjoyed this learning experience. I pray that you will take what you have learned and put that revelation into action.

As our ministry schedule permits, we offer classes in prophetic training and healing & deliverance. These classes are offered in Jacksonville, Florida usually twice a year.

Additionally, if you have a group in your city, we can come to you with a team to teach these same principles in person.

The material we teach in all of our courses is the same material contained in this book. The advantage to the classes is the activation. Half of the time of each class is spent in small groups practicing what has been taught under the supervision of a skilled coach.

You may contact us through our website at **www.Supernaturally.org**.

You may also use this secure website to make a donation to this ministry if you have received a special blessing from this book. When you give to Sozo International Ministries Incorporated, you are helping to train foreign students in the supernatural ministry of Jesus.

Most of our international ministry is in the Former Soviet Union. Because of the extremely low income level of most of the believers there, it is impossible for most to travel to come to a class, or even pay a registration fee for a local class. We provide our ministry to these believers free of charge. We travel to the foreign country, rent buildings, hire staff and produce training materials for them, all at the expense of this ministry.

Our average cost of training one Christian leader is $150. Each summer we take a team to former Soviet countries to train pastors and leaders from many different churches. We train hundreds of leaders each year.

We all believe the time available to continue this ministry is limited. Russia has already begun to evict Evangelical, Pentecostal and Charismatic ministers. For those who remain, the pressure is on. We know that one day soon, the doors will be closed for this type of training. It is vital that we make a spiritual deposit while there is a window of opportunity.

Your donation will make a difference!

May God's richest blessings hunt you down and overtake you.

Rev. Cheryl Schang

How to Keep Your Deliverance

Your deliverance is not complete- yet

1. Evil Spirits will seek to return. Jesus did not command them to go into the pit or hell Matt 12:43-33
2. When Satan tempted Jesus, he planned to renew his attacks on Jesus at an opportune time – Luke 4:13
3. When the old thoughts or feelings return, you MUST resist and rebuke the spirit. – James 4:7

Some reasons why deliverance may not be realized

1. Lack of true repentance. Repentance means a change of attitude and behavior. In the Bible the word for repentance is *Teshuva*, which means to TURN from sin and RETURN to God.
2. Failure to confess sins - 1 John 1:9; James 5:16
3. Failure to forgive others – Mark 11:25-26; Matthew 18:21-35
4. Failure to break with the occult – Acts 19:13-19
5. Unwillingness to be completely honest with God

Requirements to keep your deliverance

1. Yield every area of your life to the Lordship of Christ – John 1:11-12; Matthew 7:21-23
2. Be continuously filled with the Holy Spirit – Ephesians 5:18; Romans 8:13
3. Live by the Word of God – Luke 11:13; Matthew 4:4,7,10; Ephesians 6:17; Psalms 1:2; Psalms 119:48
4. Put on the whole armor of God by living the life that equips you – Ephesians 6:10-18
5. Cultivate a renewed mind – Romans 8:26-27; 2 Corinthians 10:3-5; Romans 8:5-7; Colossians 3:1-2
6. Pray in the Spirit – Romans 8:26-27

7. Practice praise – Isaiah 61:3; Isaiah 60:18; Hebrews 13:15

8. Cultivate right relationships – Matthew 18:15-20; 1 John 1:7, 2:9-11

9. Develop a strong dynamic faith – Romans 10:17; Mark 4:24

10. Practice confessing the Word of God – Hebrews 3:1, 4:14, 10:23

11. Seek to obey the Lord in every area of your life. IF you fail in any area, make your confession immediately – 1 John 1:9

12. Make Jesus Christ central in your life – John 12:31-32

13. Learn to know how to crucify the flesh and resist the devil – Romans 6:6, 6:11

14. Avoid those people who become a bad influence on your life – James 4:4

15. Submit to the Lord and to one another in love and humility – James 4:7, 1 Peter 5:5-6

16. Maintain a daily prayer life – Matthew 6:9-13

17. Use your weapons of defense – 2 Corinthians 10:3-5; Ephesians 6:13-18

18. Use your weapons of attack: the Word, the name of Jesus, prayer, praise, and a positive faith confession

19. Maintain a disciplined life – Romans 12:1-2; 1 Corinthians 9:27

20. Fast regularly to keep the cutting edge in your life – Matthew 6:16-18